MW00917227

RE-ENGINEER YOUR WORKDAY

CREATE TIME FOR LIFE

Rowena Hubble

BALBOA.
PRESS

A DIVISION OF HAY HOUSE

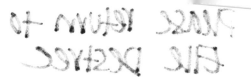

Balboa Press books may be ordered through booksellers or by contacting:

Balboa Press
A Division of Hay House
1663 Liberty Drive
Bloomington, IN 47403
www.balboapress.com.au
1 (877) 407-4847

Print information available on the last page.

ISBN: 978-1-5043-0762-8 (sc)
ISBN: 978-1-5043-0763-5 (e)

Balboa Press rev. date: 04/26/2017

To everyone who has been part of the journey of writing this book - from the inception of the idea (thank you Jacob), to the occasional prod to keep going (thank you Donna and many others), to Judi my editor and Balboa Press for publishing – thank you. To my interviewees - Stella, Catriona, Guy and Katrina thanks for your valuable insights. Most importantly to Nick, Mitchell and Layton thanks for your continual love, support and inspiration. You are the reason why I, have and continue to, re-engineer my workday to create time for life.

Contents

Introduction

We live a fast-paced, demanding life; many of us are constantly busy, often short on time, and running behind. We often feel buried in things to do and drained of the capacity to do them. We feel agitated and anxious, often stressed when we are working and stressed when we aren't. The "busyness" routine often results in us sacrificing important areas of our life, such as family, friends, physical and emotional health, in exchange for sheer hard work.

Life-work balance is something that we all desire—to achieve in the workplace without sacrificing quality time for our family, friends, interests and passions. For the majority of us, however, this is merely a dream; but, with a renewed focus on desire, productivity and effectiveness, it can be a reality.

Knowing what outcomes you want, what your highest priorities are, will enable you to focus and escape the whirlwind of activity that too often leads nowhere fast. Ask yourself: what are the important areas of your life—what is truly important to you? What do you want to be known for and always remembered for? Are these values and goals attainable, as you reflect on the reality of how you are managing your life today?

Whilst caring for people in the end stages of life, a palliative care nurse, Bronnie Ware, recorded the regrets of her patients, documented in her book, *Top 5 Regrets of the Dying*. The most stated regrets were:

"I wish I ..

1. had the courage to live a life true to myself, not the life others expected of me
2. hadn't worked so hard
3. had the courage to express my feelings
4. had stayed in touch with friends
5. had let myself be happier"

The number two regret was that they wished they hadn't worked so hard. By doing so, they had missed their children's youth and their partner's companionship. Ms Ware wrote: "The people I nursed deeply regretted spending so much of their lives on the treadmill of a work existence."

This regret is not surprising to any of us. It's a regret that perhaps you are feeling today. It was unfortunately too late for these elderly people; however, it's not too late for you.

The argument for not being able to satisfy the above wishes is often that the working days, weeks and years consume too much of our time, so we can't meet our personal desires. For many, or most of us, the obsession with work is about having enough money to meet and satisfy the material needs and wants of ourselves and our families.

So, how can we work less and still have a comfortable lifestyle? By understanding our choices and the impact those decisions have on our lifestyle, we can uncover the secrets of managing our time and energy much better. Reducing excessive hours at work is perhaps the best way to not only survive, but thrive.

We need to ask: How can technology help us? The pattern of work within the office hasn't changed significantly over many years, even with the increase in technology and connectivity. We work the same number of hours physically in the office, and even more time in peak hour traffic; but, with twenty-four-hour connectivity, we can be contacted wherever we are. Therefore, it's difficult to place limits on being engaged with work. This overwork can drain our ability to focus. So, how can we use technology to our advantage, rather than letting it be a hindrance to productivity?

We need to make the choice—the choice to get more out of the hours in the day, from the moment we wake until our head hits the pillow at the end of every day. That doesn't mean working harder; in fact, it means the exact opposite: not working harder, but working smarter. Working smarter means we value our time, making our waking hours productive and effective. This may include depositing new tools into our productivity tool kit, including setting priorities and sticking to them, creating new habits, focusing on a singular task instead of multitasking, and recognising how to maximise our energy levels.

To have it all, we do need to make some changes. These changes will ensure that we are in control and no longer constantly on the busy roller coaster of life. We have to accept that expecting to achieve a different outcome, without investing in change, will result in no change. As Henry Ford famously said, "**If you do what you've always done, you'll get what you've always got.**"

Keep in mind that nothing in this book is revolutionary. The content is commonsense and logical, but commonsense and logical in ways that aren't being practiced widely today. It's my personal guarantee that you will come away with some new tools, techniques or direction that will allow you to make some real difference in your life, allowing you to be freed from the continual busyness of life.

I challenge you to reshape your everyday routine and allow yourself to achieve all that you desire. You can't replay the key events in your life. So, manage your time and energy every day, ensuring you don't miss these opportunities.

The real secret of getting ahead is simply getting started. Let today be the start of a new tomorrow for you.

1

Challenging the 40-Hour Week

The Monday to Friday working week, from around 9 am to 5 pm, is the norm for the majority of salaried workers; and, it's been the norm for almost a century. Putting aside for now the fact that many of us work much more than the 35 to 40-hour week, why has the 9 to 5 tradition remained for so long?

If we take a look back in history, during the Industrial Revolution, factories needed to run around the clock. So, employees during this era frequently worked ten to sixteen-hour days. In the 1920s, however, Henry Ford, founder of Ford Motor Company, challenged the longer day. He was one of the first employers to establish the five-day, 40-hour work week.

The Ford Motor Company not only reduced its working day to eight hours, but it also doubled workers' pay at the same time. The shorter day coupled with a higher pay rate resulted in a spike in productivity. Within two years of implementing this change, profit margins doubled.

Moreover, Ford sought to promote an ideal home life for its employees. Company executives believed that, in order to live properly, every man should have more time to spend with his family. At Ford's own admission, however, the expectation on workers was higher with the move to the five-day work week. Although workers' time on the job had decreased, they were expected to expend more effort while they were there; and they did.

The Ford Motor Company results paved the way for other companies to adopt the shorter work day of eight hours. The paid work hours, however, have remained largely the same for most of us ever since.

Swedish Case Study

The Swedes are taking the lead in a new era of change to achieve life-work balance. Sweden has long been a laboratory for initiatives to strike a better life-work balance, recognising that treating workers well is positive for the bottom line. The six-hour work day, or 30-hour work week, has become a staple of the nation's socially progressive initiatives.

Several Swedish companies that have reduced the working day to a six-hour day have found results similar to the Ford Motor Company. The same or more work gets done in shorter time, and employees are happier. "I think the eight-hour work day is not as effective as one would think," the CEO of a Swedish app development company has commented.

"We thought doing a shorter work week would mean we'd have to hire more, but it hasn't resulted in that because everyone works more efficiently," said Maria Brath, who founded a start-up in Stockholm based on a six-hour day. "Today we get more done in six hours than comparable companies do in eight," she continued. "We believe it comes with the high level of creativity demanded in this line of work. We believe nobody can be creative and productive in eight hours straight. Six hours is more reasonable, even though we too, of course, check Facebook or the news at times."

Ms. Brath added, "Since we work fewer hours, we are constantly figuring out ways to do more with our time."

"We don't send unnecessary emails or tie ourselves up in meetings," said Thommy Ottinger, a pay-per-click specialist. "If you have only six hours to work, you don't waste your time or other people's time. It's kind of a life changer," he said, adding that the environment inspired fierce staff loyalty.

A Swedish Toyota vehicle service centre transitioned to a six-hour day back in 2002. This change was introduced to address employee stress and customer complaints concerning long waiting times. "What we can see today is that employees are, at the very least, doing the same amount in the six-hour work day, often more than they did in the eight-hour day," said Martin Banck, the service centre's director. "It's heavy work - drilling, building engine blocks - but they have stamina, and we have more profit and customers because cars get fixed faster." And employees insist that more time away from work makes them more efficient and happier on the job.

Over the span of about a year, a Swedish retirement home (Svartedalens) conducted an experiment for nurses to work six-hour days while receiving a salary for eight-hour days. This was all part of a study enacted by the Swedish government to observe whether a shorter work day might yield increased productivity on the job. A published report concluded that, in its first year, this program's six-hour work day had dramatically reduced absenteeism, as well as enhancing both productivity and workers' health.

Data from the project over a year's time, which compared Svartedalens' staff with employees of a control group at a similar facility, demonstrated clearly that sixty-eight nurses who worked six-hour days took 50 percent fewer sick days. The nurses were 20 percent happier, which is not surprising. In addition, they reported having more energy. This new-found energy allowed them to perform 64 percent more activities with elderly residents, which was one of the metrics researchers utilised to measure productivity.

Arturo Perez, an employee of the Svartedalens nursing home, was interviewed about the change. Perez says he would often come home exhausted after an eight-hour shift, caring for residents suffering from Alzheimer's. He reported having little time and energy for his three children. However, within one week of switching over to a six-hour work day, Mr. Perez had an abundance of energy. The residents of the nursing home noticed the positive impact, saying that the standard of care was higher.

"What's good is that we're happy," said Mr. Perez, "and a happy worker is a better worker."

"We've had forty years of a 40-hour work week, and now we're looking at a society with higher sick leave and early retirement," said Daniel Bernmar, leader of the Left Party on Gothenburg's City Council, which is running the trial and hopes to make it the standard. "We want a new discussion in Sweden about how life-work should be to maintain a good welfare state for the next forty years."

At Gothenburg's Sahlgrenska University Hospital, one of the largest in Europe, a similar approach has been used to counter both burnout and high absenteeism. In the orthopedics unit, eighty-nine nurses and doctors were switched to a six-hour day. The unit also hired fifteen new staff members; these employees were hired to make up for the lost time and extend operating room hours. The experiment was expensive with fifteen new hires, but it was worth it. The hospital concluded there was a dramatic reduction in employees calling in sick; and, in addition, nurses and doctors have been able to work more efficiently.

"I had reached a point where I could only work at 80 percent capacity," said Gabrielle Tikman, a surgical nurse. "Now it's easier to rest and I have time at home to sit and really talk with my children. I've got my power back." The unit reports that it is performing 20 percent more operations. Additionally, it is generating additional revenues from treatments that would have gone to other hospitals. Surgery waiting times were reduced from months to weeks, allowing patients to return to work faster, ultimately reducing sick leave in workplaces and boosting the economy.

The Swedish study isn't the first one that connected happier, rested workers and better outcomes for employers. A 2014 Stanford University research paper clarified there is a non-linear relationship between hours worked and output, stating that results start to decline after about fifty hours per week. In fact, research has shown that too much work can lead to damaged productivity.

Whilst there is strong evidence from the Swedish companies moving to a six-hour day, showing that productivity can increase with fewer hours worked, the transition to a shorter working week or even a change from the nine to five mentality, is moving very slowly. In many to most companies today, there is still the mentality that we need to be visible in the office during the nine to five working day, five days a week. Beyond the nine to five, there is a common perception that working long hours' signals dedication. It may signal dedication, in the eyes of some, but it certainly doesn't signal greater productivity.

What makes a workplace or individual successful is not the total number of hours worked: instead, it's about getting the job done. The problem is that many focus only on the "hours worked" component, and that's not the best metric for productivity.

Putting overtime aside for a moment, let's say that giving all employees the same schedule and the same number of hours may seem an equitable system. However, it presumes we are all the same, our work patterns are the same (the same each and every day) and we all need the same hours to achieve the required outcomes. The reality is that this presumption results in less than optimal productivity, decreased output, and ultimately the compromised satisfaction and happiness of employees.

Issues to Consider when We All Have the Same Schedule, Each and Every Workday:

- **Individual peak productivity** - Not everyone works the same. Some people are at their most effective first thing in the morning, but by mid-afternoon, they are ready for a long break. Others may prefer to sleep in and work later into the evening. The nine to five schedule means we all need to conform to being "on" as much as possible during nine to five.

Based on survey data, most of us reach our peak of productivity on Tuesday and experience a low on Friday. But, we are required to work the same hours each day of the week. Why not work a little longer on a Tuesday whilst productivity is high? And, on a Friday, why not finish the working day early? In reality little productive work is usually done in those last few hours on a Friday by many workers. Finishing earlier on a Friday may also be the motivator needed to accomplish more on the last working day of the week.

- **Workload variables** - There are days when ten hours are required in a work day to meet a deadline or get a task completed. Understandably, on these days, employees are expected to work overtime; and normally, they're unpaid for the extra hours. There are also other times when five hours are all that are needed to complete the day's tasks. Whilst the hours of work are adjusted for overtime, they are often not adjusted in the opposite direction—when the required output is achieved in fewer hours, there is still the expectation to work the "full" working day. This doesn't make a lot of sense.

- **Creative stimulation** - Innovation is driven by the new – new ideas, new situations, new environments and new perspectives. Creativity is challenged when the working hours and working environment each day of the week don't change.

- **Travelling time** - Travelling an hour, both to and from work, is probably close to the norm. That's 10 hours a week—or more than one full work day! Travelling is not only a big consumer of the limited resource of time, but it also can be draining mentally and physically, keeping us from achieving output—whether that is work productivity or addressing other important areas of life.

- **Distractions** - Arguably, having all employees in the office at the same time each day encourages team work and collaboration. But, this comes at the cost of distraction, whether that be idle chatter, unnecessary meetings or just general office noise from having a lot of people in a smaller space.

There are a number of alternatives to the nine to five, five-days-a-week norm that have been introduced in progressive companies. These companies are willing to shift the culture towards getting the work done, not on clocking a certain number of hours. The shift is not just when you work, but how you work and where you work. Here are a few alternatives:

- **Employees scheduling their own hours** – Employees work as they see best fit—sometimes that means working earlier, sometimes later, sometimes shorter, and sometimes longer. Implementing this requires a high level of trust to get things done and for employees to work responsibly, but if you trust your workforce and your employees are passionate about what they do, the potential benefits are limitless.
- **Less days, but more hours per day** – This won't suit everyone, but some companies and employees have moved to fitting the weekly hours in four, or even three, days.
- **Working remotely from the office** – When working from home or another location remote from the office (where the role permits), employees are free from the distractions of the office. And, they can focus on tasks, head down to accomplish more work with more autonomy and flexibility. If they are working remotely from home, the other big benefit is that they can attend to those five-minute tasks

that are required around the home during their breaks, which make a dramatic difference to their lives.

For all the benefits that flexible working brings, none of it can happen without trust. Trust is crucial—to trust employees to take accountability of their own workload and time management to get things done, whether this is at 9 am in the office or 9 pm at home. Trust already exists in every workplace today – employees are trusted with confidential business information. Why not extend this trust to allow some flexibility with work hours?

Case Study on Working from Home

Should more of us be working in our pyjamas some days? Would performance actually improve if companies let employees work from home? To understand the impact of working from home, Ctrip, a Nasdaq listed Chinese travel website company gave the staff at the company's call centre the option to voluntarily work from home for nine months. While half of the volunteers were permitted to telecommute, the rest worked in the office, serving as a control group.

Ctrip anticipated saving money on the cost of office space and furniture if employees worked from home. However, the company expected productivity would drop, based on the assumption that employees would be less disciplined when not in the office environment. Instead, those employees working from home completed 13.5 percent more phone calls than the staff working in the office did; this extra work equalled almost an extra work day a week. In addition, the at-home workers were happier, reporting much higher job satisfaction and perceived as less likely to quit.

One-third of the productivity increase was believed to be due to a quieter working environment, which makes it easier to process calls. The other two-thirds of this extra work was attributed to people at home working more hours. With no commute to work, they started their work day earlier, took shorter breaks, and worked at the end of the day at the time they would normally be commuting. Also, the number of sick days for employees working from home dropped dramatically.

One may argue that workers knew they were being monitored and measured for productivity. However, Ctrip tried to address these concerns by conducting the experiment for nine months. The positive impact of working from home was constant over that entire period, suggesting that it wasn't driven just by some initial burst of enthusiasm.

Clear evidence supports the move away from the nine to five office-based mentality. As you read through the chapters that follow, write notes and visualise how you can increase your output, but with less hours physically at your desk or perhaps the same hours but at a different start and end time.

Increased output is your greatest weapon to challenge the where and when of your working week. Less hours on the job translates to more hours for leisure. Increased output + more free time = a happy employer and a happy employee. Sounds like a formula we should all strive towards.

Check point:

- ✓ Does the nine to five norm mean you are as productive as you could be, or should you challenge the days and hours to maintain or increase output and improve your life-work balance?
- ✓ Do you spend significant time in peak hour traffic? Should you change your working hours in the office to reduce those lost commuting hours?
- ✓ How often do you work away from the office or your normal workplace? Would doing this more often assist your output?

2

My Story

For many people, there is an aha moment, a point in time, often a trigger, that forces them to reassess where they are in life. They begin to question what toll long working hours are having on their life and where to next.

My story is a little different to this scenario; there was no aha moment. For me, what started soon after leaving high school, quickly became a great habit that has held me in great stead. And, I'm proud to say that I've continued to achieve balance between home and work life to this day.

As mentioned, my journey started in my late teen years, out of sheer necessity. I was working full time and commenced my university degree. Like many part-time students, I attended university three nights a week from 6 pm to 9 pm. In order to get through university and do the best I could, which because I was a high achiever I gave myself no choice but to do, I had to get to lectures (no online lectures or internet in those days, unfortunately) three nights a week. The other nights were dedicated to assignments, study, etc. That meant leaving work on time every night. But I wanted to be a high performer at work, too. I had the belief that I could do both and made choices accordingly.

Being young and naïve, I didn't think about or probably even know the perceived culture that exists in many workplaces (and, on reflection, existed in the company I was at) that you needed to be seen in the office to climb the corporate ladder. All I knew was that I had lots of work to get done and only limited time to do it.

I soon became Miss Effectiveness, removing inefficiencies— removing so-called efficiencies that weren't effective - and, in essence, making each day as productive as possible. Not that I knew it at the time, but I was practicing the principles of the 80/20 Rule and Parkinson's Law (expanded upon in subsequent chapters). I focused on the 20 percent of effort that provided 80 percent of the productive outcomes and restricted the time I had to get the work done, and it got done.

I used the same tools and techniques from my productivity toolkit when I changed jobs part way through my undergraduate degree, and replicated the nine to five achievement. I ticked the box of graduating from University after four years with a few summer schools thrown in, to get through it in record time for a part time student. In addition, I had achieved at work, getting promoted to middle management by the time I was degree qualified.

With this recipe for achievement, why would I change my approach post graduating? Why would I revert to the all-so-familiar habits of others in the workforce of working long hours?

I continued to pack up and leave the office at 5 pm or 5.30 pm post my degree. If anyone in the office were to remark, I'd say I was doing post grad studies (which I was), or putting the finishing touches to the new house my husband and I had moved into (which I was). Externally, I occasionally needed to provide the reason why I left work on time, but internally, I knew no explanation was needed. I got through my work and more, and was living proof that you don't do a good job if your job is all you do!

I was in my mid-twenties and thought I had this balance thing all worked out, when the greatest events of my life occurred—the birth of my beautiful boys, now young men. Mitch was born first and then, two years later, Layton. And, for any parent, you know that a child will turn your whole life upside down—an incredibly positive upside down, but nevertheless upside down! Now, I not only needed to juggle work and interests outside of work, but the love, care and nurturing of two other human beings.

I was envious of the Mums or Dads who were content to take twelve months or more off work to care for their children. Unfortunately, I wasn't so content and missed the stimulation of the work environment, but yep, you guessed it: I wanted to have my cake and eat it, too. I wanted to work, but I wanted to be there for my boys. And, I didn't want to miss out on all those milestones—from newborn till today. I started working from home a lot, and worked out that, with focus, working from home can be as effective, and often more effective, than being present in the office.

When Mitch and Layton were three and one, we moved to a new home. We hadn't planned ahead for the move, and hence, hadn't planned ahead for childcare spots close to our new home (it wasn't possible to commute to the previous childcare). Finding childcare was incredibly difficult, and it was before the days of nannies other than for the very wealthy. Most centres didn't have vacancies, and for those that did, there was a reason (not a good reason) they did!

We found a suitable child care centre, but with one catch: its hours were 8 am to 4 pm. The proximity to the childcare centre, relative to work, made sense for me to do the drop off and pick up. The child care centre was only about twenty minutes from work, but that would mean a maximum work day in the office of 8.20 am to 3.40 pm. It was at that point that both I, and the company I worked for, had a tough decision to make. I either worked 8.20 am to 3.40 pm in the office or I didn't work at all.

I committed to my employer that the work would get done, and fortunately, they were willing to take the risk and see how things would go. From that day and for the next four years, I finished work at 3.40 pm each and every day (working three and then four days per week in the office), with further hours of work from home each evening.

Flexibility in the workplace is a joint partnership - requiring commitment from both the employer and the employee. There needs to be give and take to ensure the job gets done and results delivered. I ensured throughout my time of working different hours to the nine to five, five days a week, that I flexed where needed.

Two years into my 3.40 pm finish years, I was appointed Financial Controller of McDonald's Australia. At that time, I was part of the senior leadership team and had a team of about fifty employees working within my team. Yes, there were absolutely days that it was tough, really tough, to race out the office door at 3.40 pm, and it took a lot of co-ordination and discipline, but I had no choice. If I wasn't at child care at 4 pm to pick up my boys, there would be a financial penalty. But, the financial penalty was nothing in comparison to the "mum penalty," the guilt of my children thinking Mummy wasn't coming.

I'd be lying if I said there was no guilt leaving the office when my boss, my peers and my team were still working away. But guilt versus spending quality time with my children and knowing all work outcomes were being achieved – you chose?

Post the preschool days, I was adamant I wanted to be there for all those important things in my children's lives—whether that be reading groups, sports carnivals, musical performances, charity days or school community involvement. And I'm very proud to say, I've been there for most. There were days that I was torn between going to work and taking a day's leave to attend a school event. I recall someone saying: In years to come, you won't remember having attended a particular work meeting or event, but you will always remember attending that special event in your child's life. And, they will always remember you being there, too. Reflecting years later, that was great advice.

You may say I was fortunate to have the sort of job that provided flexibility; but, there were plenty around me, actually most around me, that could have made that choice themselves, but didn't. I agree that in some jobs, it's just not possible; but in most corporate roles, with lots of organisation and effectiveness, the choice is there. You know the saying 'you make your own luck.' I think this applies here, too. It's up to you.

Fast forward ten years or so—I've done a lot in the community whilst holding down demanding roles. Today, I no longer have the demands of part-time study or young children. My boys are now teenagers, but it is very rare to see me in the office past 5.30 pm. Today, the child care demands are replaced by a goal to run a half marathon, perhaps attend a school meeting, volunteer at an event, or simply to be home to have dinner with the family.

Sure, in all these years, I've done my fair share of work at night from the comfort of my home. But, it has allowed me to have it all—a career, sharing all those milestones with my family, good health, community involvement—having it all. And, I wouldn't change it for the world.

3

Less Is More

The 80/20 Principle and Parkinson's Law are two approaches to heighten productivity, with each being inversions of the other: the 80/20 Principle suggests limiting tasks to the important, so you can decrease work time and Parkinson's Law proposes defining a shorter time span for working to ensure you do restrict tasks to important ones. The best outcomes can be achieved by using both together, whereby you identify the tasks that maximise output and define very short and clear deadlines in scheduling them.

The 80/20 Principle – More Effectively Using Your Time

An Italian economist, Vilfredo Pareto, founded the Pareto principle, now known as the 80/20 Principle in 1897. Pareto observed that 80 percent of the land in Italy (and every country he subsequently studied) was owned by 20 percent of the population. Pareto's theory of predictable imbalance can be applied to almost every aspect of modern life.

Richard Koch took Pareto's Principle and applied it to business, productivity, and life. The essence of the 80/20 principle is that 20 percent of your effort accounts for 80 percent of your results. Conversely, you can apply this theory to become aware of the

80 percent of your efforts that yield only 20 percent of your accomplishments.

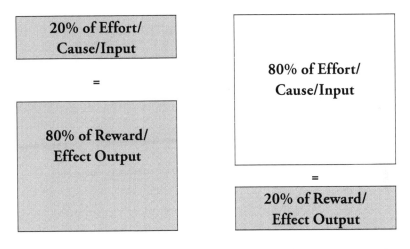

IBM was one of the earliest corporations to use the 80/20 Principle. In 1963, IBM discovered that about 80 percent of a computer's time was spent executing about 20 percent of the operating code. The company immediately modified its operating software to make the most used 20 percent very accessible and user friendly, thus significantly increasing the speed and efficiency of IBM computers relative to their competitors.

There are loads of business examples of the 80/20 Principle. This includes realising that 80 percent of a company's output is achieved by 20 percent of its employees, and 80 percent of a company's revenues come from 20 percent of its customers. It won't be exactly 80/20, but it is highly probable in business that a minority is creating a majority. It may be roughly 90/10, 70/30 or 60/40.

The 80/20 ratio applies to both your work day and your life outside work. You probably make most of your phone calls to, or spend most of your time with, a limited amount of the people you have numbers for and know. You probably wear 20 percent of your wardrobe 80 percent of the time. And, the majority of the times you eat out, you probably dine at the same 20 percent of the restaurants you know.

Results of a global six-year study with over 350,000 participants, showed there is roughly a 60/40 split (a variation of the 80/20) of time being spent on important and unimportant tasks. That is, most people spend about 40 percent of their time (that's two working days) doing tasks that don't translate into results or required outcomes. If you can reclaim even a small portion of that 40 percent, you can be amazingly more effective and productive, not to mention you can enhance the quality time you now have for family and friends.

The 80/20 Principle suggests that there is a huge amount of waste everywhere and asserts that there is no shortage of time, given we only make effective use of 20 percent of our time. The 80/20 Principle says that if we doubled our time on the top 20 percent of activities, we could achieve 60 percent more in much less time.

The 80/20 Principle: The Secret to Achieving More with Less by Richard Koch talks about the top ten low-value uses of time:

1. Things other people want you to do
2. Things that have always been done this way
3. Things you're not usually good at doing
4. Things you don't enjoy doing
5. Things that are always being interrupted
6. Things few other people are interested in
7. Things that have already taken twice as long as you originally expected

8. Things where your collaborators are unreliable and low quality
9. Things that have a predictable cycle
10. Answering the telephone/responding to emails

The idea is that much related to the above ten items makes up about 80 percent of your day, and only contributes to 20 percent of your results. You can only spend time on high-value activities, the 20 percent, if you no longer spend time on low-value uses of time. So, in order to boost your productivity, you must eliminate or substantially reduce the time you spend on the above.

"There is not enough time to do all the nothing we want to do."

— (Bill Watterson)

Do you know what you spend your hours in the office doing? Studies and data have shown that how we think we spend our time has little to do with reality. You can gain more control over your time and your work by taking one small step right now. Challenge yourself to understand what you spend 80 percent of your time on. Simply begin to look for the signs that will tell you whether you're in your 20 percent or your 80 percent. You may want to document what you do, hour by hour, for a few weeks (perhaps you could combine this with the daily activity log suggested in the chapter on Managing your Energy) to obtain clarity on your 80/20.

There is no more effective way to reduce the time taken to complete a task in your 80 percent than not doing it at all.

"Deciding what not to do is as important as deciding what to do."

— (Steve Jobs)

Too often, productivity, time management, and optimisation means we avoid the real question of whether we actually need to be doing the task at all. It's often much easier to remain busy, to work a little later on a given night than step out of your comfort zone of eliminating a task. Often, you'll have grown comfortable with doing a task, regardless of whether it's the best use of your time. As Tim Ferriss, self-help author and speaker says, "Being busy is a form of laziness—lazy thinking and indiscriminate action."

Be strong and make decisions to delete any task not leading you toward your values and your goals. A "stop doing" list is as important as a "to-do" list. By understanding what to stop doing, you can focus on the high-value items that should take up the most productive 20 percent of your time, which are, according to Richard Koch:

1. Things that advance your overall purpose in life
2. Things you have always wanted to do
3. Things already in the 20/80 relationship of time to results
4. Innovative ways of doing things that promise to slash the time required and/or multiply the quality of results
5. Things other people tell you can't be done
6. Things other people have done successfully in a different arena
7. Things that use your own creativity
8. Things that you can get other people to do for you with relatively little effort on your part

9. Anything with high-quality collaborators who have already transcended the 80/20 rule of time, who use time eccentrically and effectively

10. Things for which it is now or never

Parkinson's Law – Work Expands to Fill the Time Available for It

Parkinson's Law is the adage that "work expands so as to fill the time available for its completion," which means that if something is due next week, you will likely use the time allotted and the work will only be finished next week. If you're given two months for the same work, then the work will take two months to complete. You will mentally be "pacing" yourself based on the time you have, so even if you want to work faster, it will be mentally challenging.

Cyril Parkinson, a British historian, first observed the trend during his time with the British Civil Service. He noted that as bureaucracies expanded, they became more inefficient. He then applied this observation to a variety of other circumstances, realising that as the size of something increased, its efficiency dropped. He found that even a series of simple tasks increased in complexity to fill up the time allotted to the outcome. As the length of time allocated to a task became shorter, the task became simpler and easier to solve.

Well-known terms are the outcome of Parkinson's Law:

• If you wait until the last minute, it only takes a minute to do.

• Work contracts to fit in the time we give it.

- The amount of time that one has to perform a task is the amount of time it will take to complete the task.
- The demand upon a resource tends to expand to match the supply of the resource.

Parkinson's Law is the reason you may hear people say, "If you want something done, ask a busy person," even though this idea is somewhat paradoxical.

"The more things you do, the more you can get done."

— **(Lucille Ball)**

You are forced to complete tasks in a given time, if you are experiencing time pressure. When there is no pressure attached to a task, it will take longer to complete. In fact, the longer you have to complete the task, the longer it will take you. And, your perception of the importance of a task is influenced by the time allocated. A task that needs completion within a day isn't perceived as important, but a task that's to be finished in two months will be. Perceptions of complexity are also related to the allocated time; the more time allocated, your perception will likely be that better-quality work is required. Also, the more work your mind thinks it will take will cause you to perceive the task as overly complex and difficult. Waste thrives on complexity; effectiveness requires simplicity.

Per Timothy Ferriss in his book, *The 4-Hour Work Week*: "The world has agreed to shuffle papers between 9 am and 5 pm, and since you're trapped in the office for that period of servitude, you are compelled to create activities to fill that time. Time is wasted because there is so much time available. Since we have eight hours to fill, we fill eight hours. If we had fifteen, we would fill fifteen; however, if we had an emergency and needed to suddenly leave work in two hours, but had pending deadlines, we would miraculously complete those assignments in two hours."

If you truly focused intently, how long do you think it would take you to finish a day's worth of work? Do you think you could be done in six hours instead of eight? Maybe four? The problem is that if you have to stay until 5 pm or later, there really isn't a way for you to find out.

My early working years, and then the years to follow with young children, were spent practicing Parkinson's Law at its best. I gave myself very short deadlines due to my time constraints, and I also imposed short deadlines on those around me to coincide with my time frames. The result was that everything got done and more, in a very short time frame. If I had more time to get the work done, I don't necessarily think more would have been done.

Today, when I create self-imposed deadlines, the relevant activity/task gets done in a very short time frame. It becomes a game, a competition against the clock that I must win and I do!

Use Parkinson's Law to Your Advantage:

- Embrace deadlines and constraints! Force yourself to work against the clock.
- When you are given a task without a deadline, set the deadline yourself. I often set a deadline that I need to finish a task by 10 am, another task by 11 am, and a third task by 12 noon. I even use this principle at home; for example, I need to complete the ironing in a certain time. Without doubt, I complete the task (in this example,

the ironing) in a shorter period of time with no risk to the quality of the finished product. You will be surprised how a deadline motivates you into action, and amazed how productive you can become.

- Always state a deadline when you delegate a task to someone else.
- Deadlines should be as immediate as possible and time constraints as short as workable. The more time pressure you feel, the more focused you will be and the more work you can complete.
- Blackmail yourself: Get an accountability partner who will force you to pay up if you don't meet your deadline.

Cut your work hours in half when you sit down to plot out your day. It'll force you to be extremely picky when it comes to the tasks you agree to take on or contribute to, and it'll give you time to make sure these high priorities actually get done on time.

The overarching lesson from Parkinson's Law is that restrictions can actually create freedom. How can you add artificial parameters to your life and work, in order to become more productive and more prolific and to operate on a bigger scale?

Check point:

- ✓ **Do you know what your 80/20 is? What tasks are you spending most of your time on that are only delivering you very little benefit – both at home and at work? Would documenting your day help you understand your 80/20?**
- ✓ **What needs to go on your "stop doing" task list?**
- ✓ **What changes are you going to make today to give you more time and increase your output?**

✓ Experiment with setting tough deadlines and note the difference and enforce the same on others.

✓ Use the spare hours from getting the job done quicker to get out of the office and have fun!

4

Prioritisation

Unless you intentionally schedule time for certain work, you tend not to get to it. In order to improve this situation, each night, make it a habit to identify the most important challenge for the next day. Make this challenge your very first priority the next morning.

> **"If it's your job to eat a frog, it's best to do it first thing in the morning. And if it's your job to eat two frogs, it's best to eat the biggest one first."**
>
> — (Mark Twain)

Your "frog" is the task that will have the greatest positive impact on your outcomes at that point in time. Your frog is your **"Most Important Task" (MIT)**. You only have limited time and energy, so it's crucial you focus on completing the most important tasks that will make the biggest impact first. Do this before you spend your time and energy on anything else.

If you have two frogs, i.e. two tasks, then start with the biggest, hardest, and most important task first.

The idea is that no matter what else is going on in the day, the MITs are what you want to be sure of doing. Usually the small, unimportant tasks that need to get done every day get in the way of important tasks. However, if you make your MITs your first priority each day, the important stuff will get done instead of the unimportant.

Most of us are at our cognitive best, our brain at optimal performance, about two to four hours after we've woken up. Yet, we often waste that time on easy, relatively unimportant tasks that could be postponed to later in the day like emails, or our commute or that morning coffee run.

Combining this technique with Parkinson's Law, by setting an artificial deadline, is enormously effective. If you set a goal to finish all your MITs by X time, you'll be surprised how quickly you can complete the day's MITs.

How to find your three MITs:

1. Write down everything on your to-do list, both business as usual and project-related tasks.
2. Ask yourself: If I could only do one thing all day (and you want it to be the task that will have the greatest effect on your role), what task would I chose?
3. Move that task to your MIT list.
4. Replicate this for a second and, if needed, third MIT.

The tasks on your MIT list will stand for at least 80 percent of your output. Focus on the MITs and try to find ways to either eliminate or decrease the amount of time you spend on other tasks.

The MIT prioritisation process can be utilised beyond the work environment; it becomes useful in managing your home priorities, too.

The Eisenhower Urgent/Important Principle

Dwight D. Eisenhower, the 34th President of the United States, developed the urgent/important principle or matrix. The Eisenhower Matrix is a method of determining your MITs and prioritising other things on your to-do list.

Eisenhower's strategy for getting organised and taking action is based on separating your actions by looking at four possibilities defined by four quadrants:

Q1 - Urgent and important (tasks you will do immediately)

Q2 - Important but not urgent (tasks you will schedule to do later)

Q3 - Urgent but not important (tasks you will delegate to someone else)

Q4 - Neither urgent nor important (tasks that you will eliminate)

Q1 = Priority 1 What's urgent and important, do first.	Q2 = Priority 2 What's important but not so urgent, schedule.
Q3 = Priority 3 What's urgent, but less important, delegate to others.	Q4 = Priority 4 What's neither urgent nor important, don't do at all.

Eisenhower Matrix

According to Eisenhower, what is important is seldom urgent and what is urgent is seldom important.

Urgent tasks are things that you feel like you need to take immediate action on: emails, phone calls, texts. Important tasks are things that contribute to our values, goals and desired outcomes.

We should seek to spend most of our time on Q2 activities (important but not urgent), as they're the ones that provide us fulfillment and success. However, there are a number of key challenges to spending enough time and putting energy into Q2 tasks:

- **Knowing what is truly important to you.** If you don't know what specific values and goals matter most to you, you can't determine those tasks you should be focusing your time on for reaching those aims.
- **Present bias.** We each have a tendency to focus on whatever is perceived as the most urgent at the moment— our default mode. Motivation is a challenge when there is no looming deadline. Departing from this default position requires a good measure of willpower and self-discipline. As noted in the previous chapter on Parkinson's Law: where there is no deadline, be sure to set your own short deadline.

Given Q2 activities aren't pressing for our immediate attention, they typically keep getting put to the bottom of the pile, as we tell ourselves, "I'll get to those things 'someday' after I've taken care of the urgent things." But "someday" will never come, if you're waiting to do the important things until your schedule clears up a little. You'll always find things to do that make you too busy. In order to focus on Q2, then you need to find time—to consciously decide that you are going to make time and there will be no buts.

Quadrant 3 - Urgent and Not Important Tasks

Quadrant 3 tasks are activities requiring our attention now (urgent), but don't actually help us achieve our goals or fulfill our mission (not important). Most Q3 tasks are requests from other people, helping them reach their own goals and meet their priorities.

Examples of Quadrant 3 activities include most emails, phone calls, text messages or colleagues coming to your desk during your golden hour to ask a favour.

According to Stephen Covey (author of *7 Habits of Highly Effective People*), many people spend most of their time on Q3 tasks, thinking they're working in Q1. People feel important as Q3 tasks do help others out. They are also usually tangible tasks, which give you that sense of satisfaction as you complete them. It feels empowering to check something off your list.

While Q3 tasks help others, they don't necessarily help you. They need to be balanced with your Q2 activities. Otherwise, you'll end up feeling like you're accomplishing a lot from day-to-day, but eventually, you'll realise that you're failing to make any progress when it comes to your own long-term goals.

Quadrant 4 - Not Urgent and Not Important Tasks

Quadrant 4 activities aren't urgent and aren't important. They are primarily distractions. They include scrolling through social media, mindlessly surfing the web or watching TV. Aim to spend no more than 5 percent of your time in this quadrant.

By investing time in Q2's activities, you can eliminate much of the issues of Q1, balance the requests of Q3 with your own needs, and enjoy the time-out of Q4, feeling that you've earned Q4. By making Q2 tasks your top priority, regardless of the emergency, or deadline you're facing, you'll have the mental, emotional, and physical strength to respond positively, rather than react defensively.

Don't Prioritise the Week While You're In It – a Perfect Friday Task

Lots of offices have staff meetings on Monday mornings to priortise and plan the week; but, prioritising the week, or even just the Monday while you're in it, isn't nearly as effective as doing it ahead of time. Friday is a perfect day to talk about the coming week. You can reflect on what you accomplished over the previous week, what you want to accomplish in the next week, and you can think about what strategies you'll use to achieve that.

In addition to holding staff meetings to prioritise the week ahead, you can denote Fridays as a perfect day for individual planning and prioritisation. Ring fence an hour appointment with yourself for figuring out how to progress, track, research, strategise, or conduct any of those "thinking tasks" that normally take a back seat.

Like most, I was a Monday morning team catchup person, but now, I have made the switch to Friday. This has provided effective use of an otherwise ineffective Friday afternoon. Planning and strategising on this day versus Monday provides clarity for a productive and effective week ahead.

Learning to Say No – the Hidden Power

When we think of highly successful people, we naturally think of all the things they do. We reflect on what they are known for, but the reality is that in order for them to be successful, there would be a long list of things that they didn't do, that they said 'no' to along the way.

Our ideas of success for ourselves is often built on an impulsive habit of saying "yes" to opportunities that come our way. We're hungry for any chance to prove ourselves; and when we're presented with one, we take it. We all want to say yes because with yes comes opportunity, but with the power of no comes focus and engagement.

> **"People think focus means saying yes to the thing you've got to focus on. But that's not what it means at all. It means saying no to the hundred other good ideas that there are. You have to pick carefully. I'm actually as proud of the things we haven't done as the things we have done."**
>
> **— (Steve Jobs)**

Not knowing how to say no inevitably results in over-commitment. We wind up with a sub-standard outcome, personally exhausted and potentially hamper our reputation in the process. Research conducted at the University of California shows that the greater difficulty you have with saying no, the more likely you are to experience stress, burnout, and potentially depression.

By saying yes to too many things, we may also be saying no to some very important things.

When you feel pressured to say yes, but know that you should turn down an opportunity or request with a polite no, remind yourself of the reason behind your decision. You are not a failure if you say no. Saying no to a new commitment honours your existing commitments, and maximises the opportunity to make your current responsibility or obligation a success.

It is important to say no gracefully but firmly, maintaining the relationship with someone, while making it clear that this is one opportunity you're choosing not to pursue. Be clear on the rationale for your decision, being as transparent as possible.

There's no magic method for saying no effectively. The key is practice, practice, practice. Saying no is like any other interpersonal skill: it feels clumsy and awkward at first, and improves only with repeated effort.

Check Point:

- ✓ **Are you focused on your most important tasks? How do you determine what those tasks are?**
- ✓ **Practice the Eisenhower Matrix to get significant time back into your day.**
- ✓ **Are you saying yes to tasks or opportunities you should be saying no to? When was the last time you said yes, but should have said no? What needs to change next time?**
- ✓ **How can you make a shift to feeling okay about saying no?**

5

Starting The Day Well

"Every day, think as you wake up, 'Today I am fortunate to have woken up, I am alive, I have a precious human life, and I am not going to waste it. I am going to use all my energies to develop myself, to expand my heart out to others, to achieve enlightenment for the benefit of all beings, I am going to have kind thoughts towards others, I am not going to get angry or think badly about others, I am going to benefit others as much as I can."

— (Dalai Lama)

The Morning Routine

Quiet time in the morning is precious—that time before the outside world bleeds noise into your day. For most of us, mornings set the tone for the rest of the day. Establishing an effective morning routine sets the foundation for happiness, high energy and achievement throughout the workday.

Unfortunately, an average morning for many people doesn't start as the Dalai Lama suggests. For many, it involves hitting the snooze button multiple times, feeling incredibly time pressured, getting frustrated with others in the household, rushing out the door with little to no breakfast and arriving in the office feeling exhausted before the day even begins. Much like this scenario, is the start of your day less than ideal?

It's challenging to perform at a high level and make a significant contribution on any given day, if the start of your day is stressful. The rushed, uninspired behaviour can contribute to a negative, unproductive attitude for the remainder of the day. Making some simple changes in your morning routine can transform a specific area of your life more quickly than you would ever think possible.

The Night Before

The best morning routines begin the night before. If you want to wake up and literally bounce out of bed with enthusiasm, then you'll want to make sure you end the previous day in the best way possible.

For example, be sure to compile your to-do list the previous evening. By sorting out tomorrow's top priorities before today ends, your mind can focus on the important things to be done before you go to your job and begin work. By preparing the evening before, you know your priorities the moment you wake up.

Also, be sure to decide what clothes you'll be wearing the following day; you'll save precious time in the morning. Otherwise, you'll be standing at your wardrobe just gazing at the clothes hanging in front of you wasting precious time. To save even more time, why not select your exercise clothes too, so you can quickly put them on in the morning? Choosing these clothes the night before will encourage you to stick with your morning exercise habit!

Benefits of a Productive Morning Routine:

- **Structure and success** - One of the positive outcomes of healthy morning rituals is that you start your day with structure. This planned routine for each morning gives you direction. Morning routines that work well for you also have a positive result at the end of the day: early structure in your day allows you to enjoy some lack of structure towards the end of the day. Following a productive routine with planned discipline, and accomplishing everything you've set out to do in the earlier hours of the morning, sets you up to relax and unwind later.

- **Mental advantages** - Reflect for a moment: How different would your life be if you were consistently in a better frame of mind and had a happier disposition? According to a study by the American Psychological Association, many of us can experience great results by creating and following a better morning routine. Our stress, depression, and anxiety levels will start to decline—and our life satisfaction levels will escalate, even soar. The study reported that healthy changes caused participants to feel more motivated, and their to-do lists seemed less daunting.

- **Physical benefits** - Productive morning routines lead to improved physical benefits, as well. A harmonious beginning to your day will help you feel more energetic and strong. Additionally, when you use the morning time after you first wake up to engage in some form of exercise—a cardio workout, yoga session, or a morning walk—you'll also experience better health.

- **More quality time** - In today's world, all of us are faced with many different demands on our time. The feeling many of us have is that we are neglecting ourselves. We say, "I never have time for me!" By manipulating your morning routine to have a positive impact on your life, you'll discover this results in intentionally creating time for yourself—so you can focus on your own needs and desires.

To Improve Your Morning Routine, Try the Following Suggestions:

- **Stop telling yourself you aren't a morning person** – You may think that because you have never been a morning person that it's just not possible to change. However, you can change your underlying beliefs and gear your mindset toward making a productive morning routine a daily habit. The key lies in your mind. By deciding to overcome the invisible script of "I'm not a morning person" that you've believed for so long, you set yourself up for newfound success. According to author Ramit Sethi, invisible scripts are assumptions that are so much a part of your world view and choices that you don't question them at all. Often, there's an inner voice telling you what you should, need to, or can't do. So, if you keep telling yourself that you're not a morning person, your mind makes sure your belief is true.

- **Eat a healthy breakfast** - It's crucial to enjoy a healthy breakfast. It's considered the most important meal of the day, because it ends the overnight fasting state. Breakfast will replenish your blood sugar level by supplying glucose, which will instantly accelerate your metabolism. It also provides key nutrients essential for the energy you need to accomplish all the things you need to do. Many studies have linked eating breakfast to good health—including better memory and concentration, both needed to be productive.

- **Stop hitting the snooze button** - Comedian Demitri Martin summed up the insanity of snoozing perfectly when he said: "Hitting the snooze button in the morning doesn't even make sense… It's like saying 'I hate getting up in the morning, so I do it over and over and over again.'"

The science behind why the snooze button is bad for you - throughout the night, we experience cycles of both deep sleep and light sleep. Each cycle lasts about ninety to one hundred minutes. Deep sleep, which is more difficult to wake up from, occurs early on and dominates after falling sleep; light sleep occurs closer to one's natural waking time. It's much easier to be woken from light sleep.

It's apparent how our body rhythms could be affected by the snooze button. Each time we fall asleep, or fall back asleep, our sleep cycle starts over at the beginning. It's natural that shortly before waking, each of us should experience lighter sleep. If we were to sleep with no alarm clock, these factors would naturally allow our bodies to gradually adjust and prepare for waking.

Using an alarm clock means that we may wake in the middle of a sleep cycle, meaning our bodies haven't had time to prepare. This can easily cause an increase in sleep inertia, which most of us are very familiar with—that groggy feeling immediately upon waking. This tempts us to hit the snooze button so we can fall back asleep.

When you press the snooze button and most likely fall back asleep, this sets you up for more stress. Your sleep cycle will start over from the beginning—except this time, when your alarm goes off, you're in a deeper stage of sleep. You'll have a much harder time of waking up. The result of this new cycle is that the last portion of your sleep will become very fragmented and out of rhythm. This means you will miss out on the recovery benefits of consolidated sleep. Your ability to function effectively for the remainder of the day may be very impaired.

The best way to resist using the snooze button is to discipline yourself to create a regular sleep schedule, every day of the week. Define your exact bedtime and waking time and stick to it, even on weekends. Your body will adjust naturally after a while, and you'll find that it will be easier to wake up every morning.

Check Point:

- ✓ **Is your morning routine providing you every opportunity to perform well throughout the day?**
- ✓ **Are you planning the day ahead the evening before?**
- ✓ **Are you addicted to the snooze button?**
- ✓ **How can you improve your morning routine?**

6

Habits - We Are What
We Repeatedly Do

You first make your habits, and then your habits make you. Today, your life is essentially comprised of the sum of all your habits. For example, how in shape or out of shape you are is directly the result of your habits. Your habits determine how happy or unhappy you are. Habits directly impact how successful or unsuccessful you are. What you repeatedly do on a consistent basis (for instance, dwell on certain thoughts or participate in certain activities) will ultimately shape who you are as a person, and the type of personality you display.

How productive you are in life does not depend on discipline in isolation; rather, it also depends on making sure you form good habits. Of course, none of us are so mechanically disciplined that we automatically do all the right things all the time. But it's true that the most successful people are those who have formed good habits. These individuals aren't necessarily more intelligent or disciplined than the general population. The common denominator of those who are successful has proven to be their habits. They've invested the time to form good habits; they've devoted their time to doing the right things on a consistent basis.

If you want to achieve and maintain discipline over time, select aspects of your life that you want to apply good habits to consistently; they may be tasks you consider mundane, even boring. The secret is to 'routinise' these areas of your life so you can address them without spending a lot of time; they will happen sub-consciously. The result is the need to make fewer decisions by figuring out ahead of time how you will make these things happen.

Habit Formation

There are three phases of habit formation:

1. Making an activity a ritual
2. Turning that ritual into a routine
3. Exercising that routine until it is a habit

A ritual requires conscious effort, both for remembering to do it at all and doing it correctly. A habit just happens. Motivation will get you started; a habit will keep you going.

Here are some tips for creating a ritual, turning that ritual into a routine, and exercising that routine until it is a habit:

- **Be clear on the why** - In the words of the German philosopher, Friedrich Nietzsche, "If you know the why, you can live anyhow." In other words, when you identify a deep significance to any habit you want to acquire or goal you wish to achieve, this will encourage you to overcome the stubborn obstacles and inevitable frustrations that will get in your way.

- **Write down your reasons** - Writing down the reasons you want to form the habit or reach the goal can be very helpful. This makes your ideas clearer and helps you focus on your desired result, as well as giving you a greater sense of their reality.
- **Start with simple tweaks** - Forget trying to completely redo your life in one day. Resist the temptation to become overly motivated and plan too many changes at once. In the words of Leo Babauta, "Make it so easy, you can't say no.".
- **The two–minute rule** is geared toward the idea that by simply getting started, you can make all sorts of good things happen. These ideas can inspire you:
  - Want to eat healthier? Just eat one piece of fruit, and you'll often find yourself inspired to make a healthy salad as well.
  - Want to make reading a habit? Just read the first page of a new book, and before you know it, the first three chapters have flown by.
  - Want to train for a half marathon? Just get your running shoes on and get out the door, and you'll end up putting kilometres on your legs.
- **Make it daily** - Lasting change is a consequence of daily habits, not a magical transformation. If you want to make a habit stick, remember that consistency is critical. For instance, if you want to begin an exercise program, start going to the gym each day for the first twenty-eight days or so. Going only a couple of times a week makes it more difficult to create a habit. Activities you participate in once every few days are much trickier to keep up, making it next to impossible to form a true habit.

- **Be consistent** - The more consistently you practice a given habit, the easier it'll be to keep it up. If you want to start exercising, try going to the same place at the same time every day. If you want to form the habit of waking up earlier, set your alarm clock for the same time every morning. When mental cues like having a specific time of day, place, and circumstances are identical from day to day, it's easier to make a habit stick.

- **Record your progress** - Write your habit clearly on your calendar, so you can envision your progress with ease (seeing your progress feels good, encouraging you to take positive forward steps).

- **Associate with positive role models** - Spend more time with those individuals who exemplify the habits you want to mirror. Remember that you become very similar to what you spend time around.

- **Set a reminder** - This productive reminder to encourage yourself doesn't depend on feeling motivated, and it won't require you to necessarily remember a new habit. A good reminder makes it easy for you to start by encoding your new behaviour into something you already do. You could, for example, take a walk around the school track while you're waiting for your child to get out of school each afternoon. Setting up a highly visible reminder—such as putting your keys where you can't help but see your walking shoes, reminding you to take them with you and put them on as soon as you're on school grounds—links a new habit (walking) with a current behaviour (picking up your child). This makes it much easier to change.

- **Commit to one to two months** - You may have read that it takes twenty-eight days to make a habit; however, according to a number of studies, the time it takes to form a habit really isn't that clear-cut. Researchers from University College London examined the new habits of ninety-six people over the space of twelve weeks, and found that the average time it took for a new habit to stick was sixty-six days. Individual times ranged from eighteen to 254 days. If you want to develop a new behaviour, it will take time. You shouldn't give up if three weeks doesn't do the trick. Stick with it.

- **Reward yourself; celebrate success -** We all desire to continue doing those things that make us feel good. That's why it's important to reward yourself along the way. It's true that an action needs to be repeated to become a habit, so deliberately decide to reward yourself for successfully practicing your habit—every time, if possible.

A Great Example of the Power of Habits and Morning Routine

Well-known author John Grisham started writing his first book in 1984. At the time, he led a busy life; he worked as a lawyer and had a young family. Despite his time constraints, he had a strong belief in himself, in the power of his idea to see it through. He made the choice to fit writing a book into his life.

When he first started writing, Grisham had "these little rituals that were silly and brutal, but very important." He said, "The alarm clock would go off at five, and I'd jump in the shower. My office was five minutes away. And I had to be at my desk, at my office, with the first cup of coffee, a legal pad and write the first word at 5.30 am, five days a week. I was very disciplined about it."

His goal was to write a page every day. Sometimes that would take ten minutes, sometimes an hour; often, he would write for two hours before he had to turn to his job as a lawyer.

It took John a total of three years to finish his first novel, *A Time to Kill*. However, his method of working paid off tremendously. Since he got his first book published in 1988, Grisham has continually written one book per year. To date, he has sold more than 300 million copies worldwide. This all started with one page per day. That one positive habit done daily was the basis for changing his life.

Grisham's habits are strong; he still writes at the same place, same table, same chair, with the same cup and type of coffee each day.

There are examples like this everywhere. How can you make a new habit into a future success story for yourself?

The tools and techniques relating to productivity and increased output can become habits—so they just happen, whether it's what you do in the morning, what time you arrive and leave the office, how often you have breaks, when you check your inbox, how you prepare for a meeting...the list goes on. You can apply a habit lens to a large percentage of your life, both at work and at home.

Check Point:

✓ **Are there habits you've wanted to form, but to date you haven't succeeded? Why is that?**
✓ **What steps do you need to take to make some of your rituals into habits?**
✓ **What productivity techniques should you turn into habits? Can you start taking action today?**

7

Managing Your Energy Levels

Human energy is a renewable resource. You often hear that some people have higher energy levels than others, giving them the advantage of getting through more in a shorter time. But the truth is we all have this potential, if we can learn how to better manage our energy levels. People who seem to have limitless energy utilise their peak energy time very well, and they know when to take breaks better than others.

Our energy levels are also influenced by what we eat, caffeine consumed, sleep patterns, how hard we work, and a whole lot more. Energy capacity diminishes with both overuse and underuse. Understanding how our energy fluctuates throughout the day will allow a balance between energy consumption and energy renewal.

Know Your Golden Hours and Energy Dips

Everyone has golden hours, or biological prime time. Your golden hour or biological prime time is the window of time that you are at your peak: you're alert, ready to be productive, and intent on crossing things off your to-do list.

A crucial part of managing your energy level is maximising productivity during your peak energy time. Before you can maximise your biological prime time or golden hours, you need to understand exactly when that time is. If you aren't aware of this time, then set about finding out.

Set up a spreadsheet (example below) or create a paper form to log your daily activity. When possible, log your energy, motivation, and focus levels every two hours while awake during a two to three-week working period. Give each area a rating from one to ten. A more accurate log will result if you can resist caffeine, alcohol, and any other mood enhancers or depressants during this period. If this is not possible, ensure you note on your log when you have caffeine. Also, note when and what you eat; keep in mind that your energy will dip because of sugary, unhealthy foods that spike your blood sugar and then lower it. Logging your energy levels can be tedious, but you'll be rewarded with productivity gains after analysing the results.

Date	Time	Energy	Motivation	Focus	Time of and last food/caffeine intake
5 Sept	8 am	8	7	10	7 am cereal, toast
5 Sept	10 am	10	7	10	-
5 Sept	Noon	8	6	6	
5 Sept	2 pm	6	6	6	1 pm sandwich, fruit
5 Sept	4 pm	4	4	4	-
5 Sept	6 pm	4	4	4	-
5 Sept	8 pm	2	2	2	7 pm dinner
6 Sept	8 am	9	8	9	7 am cereal, toast

After two to three weeks of keeping your log, you should see trends during your day. Whenever your energy, focus, and motivation align at a high point, you've found a biological prime time or golden hour. Energy spikes, however, aren't a good thing when they're followed by a crash (like when you've consumed a lot of caffeine or sugar).

Once you find your best time, protect it with all your might; this frees you up to do your best, uninterrupted work. Where possible, block the time out in your calendar as often as you can and use these high-energy hours for your highest priority tasks—especially those that require more mental energy and focus.

Once you have a sense of your prime time, you can then mould your schedule so that the activities you need less energy for (e.g. checking emails) are scheduled in your low energy times. Plan to take a break when your energy dips, so you can recharge.

Working All Day Without a Break is Counterproductive - We Need To Renew Our Energy Levels

Whatever the work practice or schedule, our brains are designed to work in roughly the same way—in periods of time following a natural flow of energy peaks and troughs. Known as our ultradian rhythm, discovered by Nathan Kleitman, this energy cycle of 90–120 minutes takes us through different levels of alertness.

Peak alertness

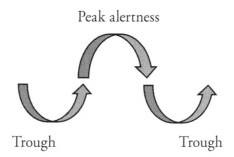

Trough   Trough

Energy cycle 90-120 minutes
(Ultradian Rhythm)

It's true that our bodies slowly transition from a high-energy state into a physiological trough. The body requires a period of rest and recovery toward the end of each cycle. We all experience the signals it's time to renew; those signals include feeling restless, needing to yawn, feeling hungry, and having difficulty concentrating. However, many of us try to ignore these signals and keep on working. The consequence is that our energy reserves, our remaining capacity to cope, will erode as the day goes on.

By choosing to work in sync with this natural flow of energy, we can increase our productivity and efficiency by limiting our periods of focus. Intermittent breaks for renewal let us give a more sustainable, increased effort in our activities. The length of time taken for refreshing ourselves is less important than the quality of that rest. It's possible to gain a great deal of recovery and rest in a short time, if you practice a ritual that allows you to fully disengage from work. In other words, the ritual must allow you to truly switch channels. That positive switch might range from engaging in small talk with a colleague about something other than work, to listening to music, to taking a walk up and down the stairs or around an office building. While many organisations consider taking breaks to be countercultural, and they are counterintuitive for many high achievers, their value is multifaceted.

There are three scientific reasons for prioritising breaks while at work:

1. **Breaks prevent boredom, and make it easier to stay focused**. That's because the human brain wasn't built for the type of extended focus we demand of it all day. The fix for this unfocused condition is easy; all we need to get back on track is a brief interruption.

51

2. **Breaks assist information retention and forming mental connections.** Our brains have two modes: focused mode (which we use when we're doing things like learning a new skill, writing a document, or working intently) and diffuse mode (which is our more relaxed, day dreamy mode). We are in this mode when we're not actively thinking too hard. Most of us might believe the focused mode will help us optimise productivity, but being in diffuse mode is critical in balancing how our brain works.

   We used to believe our brains went dormant when daydreaming. However, recent studies show just the opposite; there is increased activity in many brain regions, when we allow our minds to wander. Some studies have shown something very interesting happens that we wouldn't expect, but you've most likely experienced: the mind solves its toughest problems while daydreaming. While you're in the shower or driving along, you may suddenly resolve an issue. Breakthroughs seemingly coming from nowhere can often result from diffuse mode thinking. Diffuse mode thinking occurs when you are taking a true break.

3. **Breaks help us re-evaluate our goals.** What happens is this: when you concentrate on a task continuously, it's easy to lose focus. You get lost as you're pulled into the details of the work in front of you. In contrast, if you stop for a brief break, you can pick up right where you stopped before. This forces you to spend a little time thinking holistically about your project. You begin to ask yourself if you're on the right track to getting the work done. It's a

practice that ensures we take a break to review our results. We are encouraged to be mindful of our true objectives.

What doesn't get planned usually doesn't get done, so make sure to plan for breaks. Better still, make them a habit—then they will just happen.

Check Point:

✓ **Do you know your golden hour/biological prime time?**
✓ **Do you manage your day so that you use your prime time for high priority tasks, and down time for less mentally challenging tasks?**
✓ **How often do you have a break throughout the day?**
✓ **How can you introduce more breaks into your day and make them a habit?**

8

Happiness Makes A Difference

There's a clear link between happiness at work, your positivity level, and the productivity and success of you and your team. No system, tool, or methodology can beat the productivity boost you get from your attitude. Your attitude directly impacts your ability to get work done. The link is obvious, but there is also substantial research proving that happier employees are more productive in the workplace.

A 700-person experiment was conducted in Britain by the Social Market Foundation and the University of Warwick's Centre for Competitive Advantage in the Global Economy. Researchers chose individuals at random, and either showed them a ten-minute comedy clip or provided them with snacks and drinks. They then followed up with a series of questions to ensure that the "happiness shocks," as they're referred to in the report, actually made the subjects happy. When it was confirmed that they did, the researchers gave them tasks to measure their levels of productivity.

The experiment showed that productivity increased by an average of 12 percent, and reached as high as 20 percent above the control group. Dr Daniel Sgroi, the author of the report, concluded: "Having scientific support for generating happiness-productivity cycles within the workforce should help managers to justify work practices aimed at boosting happiness on productivity grounds."

The Harvard Business Review completed an analysis of hundreds of studies showing the positive benefits of happiness, including, on average: 31 percent higher productivity; 23 percent fewer fatigue symptoms; 37 percent higher sales; three times higher creativity and ten times more engagement. All very compelling results.

Below is a summary of scientific research findings that support the idea that having a positive attitude makes you more productive. A positive attitude:

- **Enhances your problem-solving skills** - Positive thinking extends your scope of attention, which enhances problem solving. With a negative attitude, you tend to focus on the problem; it becomes difficult to fix, and negativity often multiplies the issue. A positive attitude can turn a bad situation around. When you are happy, you just fix it. Your mind is more open to possibilities, making it easier to solve problems.

  A research study by The National Center for Biotechnology Information in the United States found that when people were presented with a task, those who had seen a positive video before performing the task did a better job and were more open to solving problems than those who watched an angry or depressing video.
- **Improves decision making** - A positive, happy attitude equals a clearer mind, allowing you to take appropriate action and make more informed decisions—instead of reacting to your emotions.

- **Improves teamwork** - Nothing brings a team together and builds relationships like positivity. Happy, positive people are a lot more pleasurable to be around, have an easier time bonding with others and working in teams, and have better work relationships. This results in greater productivity and success for all.

  People who think positively are more open to trusting others and research studies have also proven that smiling makes it easier for other people to trust you. The more you trust other people, the easier it is to work in a team, because you're open to discussing ideas and building on those ideas collectively.

- **Boosts creativity** - There appears to be a cognitive process that kicks in when we feel good that naturally leads to more flexible, fluent, and original thought processes. There's also a carryover, known as the incubation effect, to the very next day. If an individual is in a good mood on a particular day, they'll be more likely to experience creative ideas that day and the next. This is true for the next day even when a mood change is taken into account (according to a study conducted by Teresa Amabile, Baker Foundation Professor and Director of Research at Harvard Business School).

- **Helps maintain a high-energy level** - It's often true that people with a positive attitude have more energy. You'll find that when you think positive thoughts and smile, this results in endorphins being released, which will increase energy. Having more energy means you can accomplish more, increasing your overall productivity.

- **Increases brain stimulation and reduces stress** - People who maintain a positive attitude smile more. In an article posted on TedTalk.com titled, The Hidden Power of Smiling, Ron Gutman reveals how studies have found that smiling is known to increase brain activity. The more positive thoughts you experience, and the more you smile, the better your brain will function.

Here's another benefit: It's been proven that smiling reduces stress. Stress clouds your mind and will certainly weigh you down, whereas focusing on thinking positive thoughts and smiling a lot reduces stress. The result of this is that you'll find it's easier to focus and get things done.

Does being productive automatically make us happy, or does being happy play a role in our productivity? It works either way, but studies have shown the correlation is most powerful when starting with happiness (thinking in a positive way and smiling on purpose) translating into productivity. This means that if you want to be more productive, the best approach is to focus on being happy as you perform your tasks and strive to reach your goals.

Here are some happiness habits. How many are you practicing today?

- Show kindness to other people
- Forgive often
- Appreciate more
- Live in the present
- Practice acceptance
- Exercise
- Dream big
- Make time to play
- Take time to recharge

- Give yourself a treat
- Congratulate yourself
- Care for yourself
- Smile and laugh whenever possible

Check Point:

✓ **Do you generally have a positive or negative attitude at work? Are you aware of how this impacts your productivity?**

✓ **What can you start or stop doing today to make your days happier and allow you to get through your day more effectively?**

9

Focus

**When you focus on what you want,
everything else fades away**

The ability to focus on what really matters, efficiently and effectively, is an essential attribute for success. We need the ability to ignore the multitude of distractions that work to pull us away from the task at hand.

By focusing all your attention on just one thing, you can give it the attention it needs, and you will get results.

We need not only to focus, but also to fix that focus and narrow it like a laser to an attention span that remains constant and unwavering—to immerse ourselves completely in the task. Immersing oneself completely in a task is called flow.

Flow can be defined as the mental state one operates in that causes a person to perform an activity fully engaged with a feeling of being energised. This means the individual has energised focus. He or she is completely involved with the work or activity at hand, enjoying the process of it all. The essence of this is characterised by complete absorption in the activity, during which a person feels the flow and doesn't notice much else. Mihály Csíkszentmihályi has named this state of achieving flow in colloquial terms as "being in the zone."

According to Csíkszentmihályi some of the challenges related to remaining in flow include states of apathy, boredom, and anxiety. A state of apathy arises when challenges are low and a person's level of skills are also low; this results in a general lack of interest in the task at hand. Boredom is somewhat of a different challenge. This occurs when challenges at hand are low, but one's skill level far exceeds those challenges—causing one to look for enhanced challenges. Lastly, a state of anxiety happens when challenges are so high that they go beyond a person's perceived skill level, causing distress and a state of uneasiness. Overall, these states differ from being in a state of flow, in that flow occurs when challenges match one's skill level. Csíkszentmihályi has said, "If challenges are too low, one gets back to flow by increasing them. If challenges are too great, one can return to the flow state by learning new skills."

We live in an age of distraction; yet one of life's paradoxes is that our brightest future hinges on our ability to pay attention to the present. We need to starve distractions and feed our focus.

Social media, along with other types of digital distractions, don't interrupt us if we close out of them and learn to focus ourselves fully on the task before us. If we need to spend time on email or text others, we can put aside everything else and just be fully focused on that single digital task.

If your job demands that you totally focus on a task defined as urgent, you may stress out because you have a million other things to do. Your time is very limited, and you don't have time to do everything. Or, you can choose to be present, focusing fully on that task. And now there is only that one task before you. When you're done, you can simply move forward to the next task.

Being present is a good option for managing any problem. It's a way to more easily handle any problem, any distraction, or stressful situation at hand. This focus on your part allows everything else to fade away, leaving only you and any tasks you're dealing with right now.

Focusing on the present has a lot of great benefits. It allows you to stay calmer in a stressful environment or situation. It allows you to put limits on time spent allowing your mind to wander, from thinking about the past and regrets to dwelling on the future and feeling anxious about situations that haven't even occurred yet. Focus permits concentration on the one area you can truly control: the present. Focusing on the present increases your productivity and your effectiveness overall.

Concentrating on the now, rather than the past or the future, isn't easy though; it takes some practice. If you practice being present on a regular basis, similar to other tasks, you become increasingly proficient at it. It eventually becomes a mode of being, not just a task on your list.

Most people don't learn to be fully present. This isn't because it's hard to do, but due to the fact that they don't practice. Practice, more practice, and being present will become natural. Here are some ways to practice focusing on the present:

- When you eat, just eat. Pay attention to what you're eating, and do it slowly. The same applies to other activities such as driving and washing dishes. Don't try to do multiple things at once—just do what you're doing now, and nothing else.

- Become more aware of your thoughts. Most likely, you will think about the past and future—that's okay. Awareness will bring change.
- Try meditation. Meditation is a practice that lets an individual train the mind or induce a different mode of consciousness, either to realise some benefit or for the mind to simply acknowledge its content without becoming identified with that content. Anything that quietens your racing thoughts can be your form of meditation: exercise, a repetitive task like washing dishes, or a soak in the bath, as examples.

Check Point:

- ✓ Are you conscious of when you need focus, but you're just not getting into the flow?
- ✓ What is stopping you from focus – is it the environment, a digital device, your energy level or combination of challenge and skill?
- ✓ How can you practice being present?

10

Belief

"Your beliefs become your thoughts,
Your thoughts become your words,
Your words become your actions,
Your actions become your habits,
Your habits become your values,
Your values become your destiny."

— (Mahatma Gandhi)

The strength of our beliefs is the foundation of performance and success, whether that be at work, on a sporting field, or in any other area of our lives. If you believe you can do something, you're halfway to the finish line; if you believe you can't do it, you aren't even at the starting line.

In the early years of my career, I believed I could achieve at work without working long hours. When childcare became a challenge, I believed I could make it work by working different hours than the typical nine to five. My belief shaped my habits and allowed me to achieve the balance I desired.

While training for a half marathon, I lost the belief that I could do it. As a result, I just couldn't go the distance. When that belief returned, without doing anything else differently, I could suddenly make the distance. Without belief, you just won't get there. With belief, you give yourself every chance possible.

"Whether you think you can, or think you can't, you're right."

— (Henry Ford)

The self-fulfilling prophecy 'believe it and you'll achieve it' is as alive and well today as it was yesterday and will be tomorrow. We are all born with no sense of what we can or can't do. You will never hear a young child say, "I'm not the kind of person who could..." Our beliefs are acquired one by one along life's journey. During our lives, we limit our horizons through what we learn or are exposed to.

The good news is that with time, we can change our beliefs. Just like we learn our limiting beliefs, we can also alter them and learn stronger self-belief.

We need to be aware of our self-beliefs and work towards strengthening our own beliefs. Here are some ideas for increasing your self-belief:

- **Set bold but realistic goals** - The achievement of a goal will build your self-belief. You can then gradually aim higher; and, with each subsequent step forward, you will build your self-belief. Whether you want to lose weight, join a fun run, or climb the corporate ladder, the concept is the same; set a goal that's maybe a bit daring, but realistic enough for you to believe in it.

- **Focus on positive self-talk** - If self-doubt or self-criticism creeps in, challenge it, ignore it or turn up the volume on your positive self-talk to drown it out.

"If you hear a voice within you say 'you cannot paint', then by all means paint and that voice will be silenced."

— (Vincent Van Gogh)

- **Be your own motivational coach** - When you doubt yourself, consider what you would say to someone whom you really believed in if they were having doubts. Sit quietly and say the same things to yourself.
- **Learn to see your accomplishments** - Consciously work on identifying and acknowledging your strengths and achievements, big and small. Spend some time each day thinking about them. This will help you see yourself differently.
- **Continually develop yourself** - Be a life-long learner, and continually aim to better yourself. Self-belief is a reflection of your ability to handle the various aspects of life. The more you grow as a person, the more reasons you have to believe in yourself.
- **Reduce the comparisons between yourself and others** - It's inevitable that no matter how amazing you are, you will always find somebody who is better than you at something. It's human nature to compare, but keep your mind busy on other things to reduce the comparison time. Be conscious of when you start to compare, and divert your mind elsewhere.

- **Give yourself an unlimited number of opportunities to be successful** - The only true failure is when you give up.

Psychologist Albert Bandura conducted a study that showed the role of attitudes in the presence of failure. Two groups of study participants were required to complete an identical management task. The first group was informed that the purpose of the task involved measuring their management ability. It was explained to the other group that the skills needed to finish the task were simply to be enhanced—that the task was simply an exercise for practicing skills they needed to improve upon. The researchers set up the task in such a difficult fashion that all participants would fail, so of course they all did. The first group, feeling like failures because their skills weren't adequate, made little or no improvement when given opportunities to repeat the task. The second group, however, perceived each of their failed attempts as a learning opportunity. Oddly enough, they performed at progressively higher levels each time they attempted the task. As far as the second group's perspective of themselves from this experiment, they rated themselves as having more confidence than the first group did.

The now-famous individuals listed below started out as your typical brothers, sisters, sons, daughters...people from any neighbourhood. They received their fair share of setbacks, but staying true to their self-belief, they persisted—the results speak for themselves:

- **J.K. Rowling** had all twelve major publishers reject the Harry Potter manuscript. Later the same year, a small publishing house accepted it: Bloomsbury. Today, Rowling's books have sold more than 400 million copies. She is known as the most successful woman author in the United Kingdom.

- **Walt Disney** was fired by an editor due to lack of imagination and having no good ideas. His first company also ended in bankruptcy.
- **Abraham Lincoln** was demoted in the army, had several business failures, and lost eight times when he ran for public office.
- **Thomas Edison** failed to invent the lamp 999 times before he succeeded on the 1000th attempt.
- **Bill Gates'** idea of creating a computer that had a graphic interface and a mouse was rejected when he first submitted these ideas to another company. Stories suggest that the papers detailing the project were thrown in his face.
- **Winston Churchill**, the Nobel Prize-winning, twice-elected prime minster of the United Kingdom struggled in school and failed the sixth grade. After school, he experienced years of political failure, defeated in every election for public office before finally becoming prime minister at the age of sixty-two.
- **Michael Jordan**, one of the best basketball players in history, started out by being cut from his high school basketball team. Luckily, Jordan refused to let this setback put the brakes on his career. He has said, "I have missed more than 9,000 shots in my career. On twenty-six occasions, I have been entrusted to take the game winning shot, and I missed. I have failed over and over and over again in my life. And that is why I succeed."

In addition to our self-belief we need to realise that our personal success is also impacted by others around us. Their beliefs about us affect our outcomes.

The Pygmalion Effect, or Rosenthal effect, can be defined as: the phenomenon whereby higher expectations of any individual will lead to an increase in performance by that person. A corollary of the Pygmalion effect is the Golem Effect. This is a phenomenon whereby low expectations of someone lead to a decrease in performance; from a psychological standpoint, both are forms of self-fulfilling prophecy.

Our action towards others impacts **others beliefs (about us)** which causes **others actions (towards us)** which reinforces **our beliefs (about ourselves)** which influences **our action towards other** and the cycle continues.

The idea behind the Pygmalion effect is this: increasing any leader's expectation of the follower's performance will automatically result in a better performance by that follower. Within the field of sociology, the effect is often cited with regard to education and social class.

Robert Rosenthal and Lenore Jacobson's study of the Pygmalion Effect showed that if teachers were led to expect an enhanced performance from their students, their performances were improved. This study supported the hypothesis that true outcomes, the reality of an individual's efforts, can be positively or negatively influenced directly by the expectations of other people. Rosenthal argued that biased expectancies targeted toward certain subjects could affect reality, and create self-fulfilling prophecies regarding those people.

The study involved all students in a single California elementary school being given a disguised IQ test at the beginning of the study. Teachers were not given these scores, but were informed that some of their students (about 20 percent of the school, a percentage chosen at random) could be expected to be "intellectual bloomers" that year. These individuals would do better than expected in comparison to their classmates. The bloomers' names were given to the teachers. At the end of the study, a test was given again to all students in the school (the same IQ test used at the beginning of the study). First and second graders showed statistically significant improvements that favoured the experimental group of intellectual bloomers. This led to the study's conclusion that a teacher's expectations, particularly for the very youngest students, can influence overall student achievement. Rosenthal believed that even attitude or mood could have a definite, positive effect on students, when a specific teacher was made aware of the bloomers. In fact, in times of difficulty, it was concluded that the teacher may pay closer attention to that child, and even treat the child differently. Rosenthal made a prediction that elementary school teachers may subconsciously behave in ways that facilitate the student's success.

The teaching example can also be applied to the workplace. You can put this theory into practice by surrounding yourself with people who have high expectations of you. Their belief in you will subconsciously lift your performance.

Check Point:

- ✓ **How strongly do you believe in your life and work goals?**
- ✓ **How can you strengthen your self-beliefs, starting today?**
- ✓ **What do others expect of you? How can you surround yourself with people who have high expectations of you?**

11

Multitasking

Multitasking, many would argue, is a necessity in the face of all the demands we need to juggle in today's society. In our highly-connected and fast-paced world, we are constantly flooded with information. It's not unusual to be answering emails, phone calls, and texts almost simultaneously. Of course, you want to reply to all instantaneously, but you'll pay a price.

Multitasking is a physiological impossibility, unless you happen to be in the one to two percent of the population who are "supertaskers" and use different parts of their brain to divide attention. Your brain most likely can only concentrate on one thing at a time. When you try to accomplish two tasks simultaneously, your brain doesn't have the capacity to complete both tasks successfully.

Experiments have demonstrated that the problem doesn't arise from doing two things at once, so much as doing two separate, conscious mental tasks at once. This results in a significant drop in performance. This suggests that completing multiple tasks is possible without impacting performance—if all but one of the tasks are done subconsciously (habitually). For example, when you drive a car you are multitasking—but using the accelerator, braking, putting your indicator on, etc. are routine tasks for an experienced driver. This is very different if you are learning to drive, though. A learner driver hasn't been driving long enough for any of the tasks related to driving a car to be routine; each time they add a task, their performance will be impacted. For instance, if the first task is accelerating, and a learner driver then needs to put their indicator on, it is likely they will initially either take their foot off the accelerator or put it down too hard when needing to multitask.

When it comes to having an attention span and the ability to be productive, our brains have a finite capacity. Contrary to popular belief, our brains are not wired for multitasking well. It's like a pie chart with one section much larger than the others; whatever we're working on will consume most of that pie. There isn't a lot left over for additional tasks, with the exception of automatic behaviours or sub-conscious tasks such as walking. Switching back and forth between several tasks actually reduces productivity, and wastes time. This is due to the fact that your attention is expended on the act of switching gears—plus, the reality is that you never get fully "in the zone" for either activity. Experts estimate that switching between tasks can cause up to a 40 percent loss in productivity.

This constant switching back and forth on tasks encourages bad brain habits. When we finish a small activity (sending an email, answering a text message), we are hit with a dollop of dopamine, which is our reward hormone. Our brains love that dopamine, so we're tempted to keep switching back and forth between mini-tasks that provide lots of instant gratification. This leads to a dangerous feedback loop. This situation makes us feel like we're accomplishing a lot, but the truth is, we're not really doing much at all (at least nothing that requires much critical thinking).

Stanford researchers compared various groups of people in a study based on individuals' tendency to multitask and each person's belief that multitasking helps their performance. Researchers discovered that people who heavily multitask—those who engage in it often, and feel this practice enhances their performance—were actually worse at multitasking than others who preferred to accomplish one thing at a time. The frequent multitaskers performed worse because this group had more trouble organising their thoughts. They also had trouble filtering out irrelevant information, in addition to being slower at switching from a given task to another.

People who are busy trying to do two or more things at once don't even see obvious things that are clearly apparent to others. We witness this every day, particularly given the addiction to mobile phones. According to a 2009 study from Western Washington University, 75 percent of college students who were observed walking across a campus square and simultaneously talking on their cell phones failed to notice a nearby clown riding a unicycle. Researchers refer to this as "inattentional blindness," saying that despite the fact the individuals using phones were technically looking at their surroundings, none of it actually registered in their brains. This may have been okay in the case of not seeing the clown but it can have more serious consequences in the workplace and in society generally.

It makes sense that if you try to accomplish two things at the same time, such as read a book and watch television, you will miss important details of one or both activities. But even stopping one task to suddenly concentrate on another can be sufficient to disrupt one's short-term memory.

Multitasking utilises working memory, or temporary brain storage. When our working memory is fully used up, it can subtract from our ability to think creatively, according to research from the University of Illinois at Chicago. Researchers suggest that, with too much activity already going on in their minds, multitaskers will often find it difficult to daydream and generate spontaneous "ah-ha" moments.

OHIO is an acronym for 'only handle it once,' meaning you take something on and don't quit until you've completed it. The problem with multitasking, however, is that it generally makes OHIO impossible—instead, you're handling each thing multiple times. And every time you do, you'll be psychologically switching gears. This constant switching requires as much time for you to resume performing a major task that has been interrupted as you've spent working on it, if not more. In their book, *The Cost of Not Paying Attention: How Interruptions Impact Knowledge Worker Productivity*, Jonathan Spira and Joshua Feintuch state that more than 25 percent of every nine to five workday is taken up by such interruptions.

Multitasking makes it more difficult to get our thoughts organised, and it's harder to filter out irrelevant information. This reduces the efficiency and quality of anyone's work. Research reveals that in addition to slowing down our efforts, multitasking lowers your IQ temporarily. A study at the University of London found that participants who multitasked during cognitive tasks experienced IQ score declines similar to what they'd expect if the subjects had smoked marijuana or stayed up all night. IQ drops of fifteen points for multitasking men ended up lowering their scores to the average range of an eight-year-old child. So, the next time you're writing an email to your boss during a meeting, keep in mind that your cognitive capacity is being diminished significantly; you might as well let an eight-year-old write the email for you.

The biggest impact of multitasking mayhem comes from our inboxes. Some studies demonstrate that even having the potential opportunity to multitask, such as thinking about an unread email in your inbox, can lower your effective IQ by ten points! Having the constant thrill of a new, bolded email in our inbox can keep us perpetually distracted. Email is problematic, but texting is even worse. Texting demands much more immediacy than email, tempting us to check it more often. How many hundreds of touches a day does your mobile or cell phone receive?

Multitasking has also been proven to increase the production of cortisol, referred to as the stress hormone. Having our brain constantly switch gears pumps up our stress level and tires us out, causing us to feel mentally exhausted (despite the fact the workday has barely begun).

Multitasking is certainly not a skill one should include on a resume; instead, it should be considered a bad habit that one should put a stop to. We all need to turn off notifications on our computers, create specific times to check email during the day, and put our focus on the task before us.

Refer to the chapters on prioritisation, habits, focus and managing your inbox for tips on how to move away from multitasking.

I'm a self-confessed multitasker. After doing research for this book, I've started to take notice of things I do and how multitasking is letting me down. I am changing, but the change is slow. There are years of the task-switching habit that I need to change. The change to date however, has already had positive impact on my productivity.

Check Point:

- ✓ Be more conscious of when you multitask, and notice how it impacts your performance.
- ✓ Consciously reduce multitasking, one task at a time.
- ✓ Use the ideas from the chapter on focus to help you make the shift away from multitasking.

12

Procrastination

"This constant, unproductive preoccupation with all the things we have to do is the single largest consumer of time and energy."

— (Kerry Gleeson)

You are who you are because of either motivation or procrastination. By allowing yourself to put things off, you are likely dealing with an impact that can have greater implications than you realise. To begin with, it fosters distress. Besides the presence of stress and guilt that are connected to procrastination, consider the other consequences of putting off what you need to do, such as earning a bad reputation with colleagues, friends, and family—and losing your ambition to succeed and failing to accomplish your dreams.

Procrastination makes easy things hard and hard things harder. Imagine all the things you'd accomplish if you never procrastinated.

You procrastinate when you ignore and delay tasks that you should be concentrating on at the moment. This is usually done in favour of taking on something that brings more enjoyment, or an activity or task that you're more comfortable doing. According to psychologist Professor Clarry Lay, a prominent writer on this particular subject, procrastination occurs when there's "a temporal gap between intended behaviour and enacted behaviour." The bottom line is that procrastination involves a significant amount of time between when people intend to do a job, and when they get around to actually doing it.

Procrastination is common, yet we may not even realise we're doing it. When we unknowingly act like an avoider, we create various reasons in our minds for delaying a given task at hand—sometimes indefinitely. To stop this type of avoidance behaviour, we have to recognise it as procrastination. Facing the facts is half the battle in stopping this approach to work and life. Here are some indicators to help you identify times when you're procrastinating:

- Your daily schedule is full of low-priority tasks from your to-do list.
- You read e-mails several times, without answering or deleting them—or even deciding what you want to do with them.
- You sit down to focus on a task you'd classify as high priority, but almost immediately get up to make yourself a cup of coffee.
- A specific item is still on your to-do list after a long period of time, even though you know it's important.
- You regularly agree to those unimportant tasks other people are asking you to do, spending your time on them instead of moving forward with important items already on your list.
- You wait until you're in the "right mood" or it's the "right time" to tackle an important job. You may tell yourself you need a specific amount of time, physical space, equipment, or whatever, then wait for everything

to come together magically. Oddly enough, the magic rarely shows up!

Adopt Anti-Procrastination Strategies

Procrastination is an ingrained habit, so you can't break it overnight. Bad habits only come under your control when you have persistently stopped practicing them. So, use as many approaches as possible to maximise your chances of defeating them.

As Sir Isaac Newton taught us a very long time ago, objects at rest tend to remain at rest and objects in motion tend to stay in motion. This applies to humans just as well as it does to falling apples. Here are some general tips to get you going and keep you moving:

- If the task takes less than two minutes, do it now.
- If the job seems overwhelming, break the project up into a set of smaller, more manageable tasks. Break it down into little parts, then focus on one part at a time. If you still procrastinate on the task after breaking it down, break it down even further.
- Begin with some quick, small tasks if you can, even if logically these don't seem like the initial actions to take. By just starting something, you'll feel that you're achieving things—so perhaps the whole project won't seem so overwhelming after all.
- Make a smart to-do list by writing down only the tasks that you're avoiding, not the ones you know you'll do anyway. Then back this up by defining deadlines.
- Identify the unpleasant consequences of not completing the task. Come up with a consequence that will deter you from putting it off.

- Stop waiting for the perfect time; there's never a perfect time. Think of a task/project you undertook and performed perfectly with no mistakes at all. Hard to think of something? If you keep waiting for one, you're never going to accomplish anything. Perfectionism is one of the biggest reasons for procrastination. No matter how inexperienced, uneducated, or unprepared you might feel, right now is the best time to jump into action.
- Make your intentions public. It's a great way to keep yourself accountable to your plans. This will add pressure. For some of us, avoiding embarrassment is the mightiest motivator.
- Set a time to complete a task, so that you have no time for procrastination.
- Reward yourself for finishing the task.
- And lastly, act. Do it! Get on with it. You can strategise, plan and hypothesise all day—but if you don't take action, nothing will happen.

The longer you can avoid procrastination, the greater your chances of stopping this negative habit for good will be! The best way to get something done is to begin.

Check Point:

- ✓ **Recognise when you are procrastinating.**
- ✓ **What tips can you use to minimise procrastination?**
- ✓ **What price will you pay if you fail to accomplish delayed tasks versus enjoying the feeling of reaching specific goals you've been putting off?**

13

Manage Your Inbox So It Doesn't Manage You

Do you always begin your day reading emails, thinking that you'll only respond to the most important ones—then finally look up and realise an hour or more is gone? Without focused management, our inboxes can take a lot of time and energy, making us feel that we struggle to just keep our heads above water.

On average, each of us spends over a quarter of our day wading through our inbox (28 percent per a McKinsey Global Institute Study). That's a huge opportunity cost on our time.

It's not enough to be efficient with your inbox if your efficiency is ineffective. Efficiency is performing a given task (important or not) in the most economical manner possible. Checking emails thirty times throughout the workday and creating a system of folder rules and sophisticated techniques for ensuring that you move them out of your inbox as quickly as possible may be efficient, but it's far from effective.

Here are some tips to allow you to manage your inbox more effectively and get significant time back in your day.

- **Turn off your new mail alert** - The intention of the alert is to let you know there is another new email in your inbox. This may have been relevant when there was very little email traffic, if that was ever the case. However, now we all receive emails constantly and consistently through the day. The alert is doing nothing more than highlighting the obvious reality, but it is killing your productivity. Every time you receive an alert, it distracts you from the task at hand. Turn it off and you'll instantly see a difference.

- **Establish a schedule for checking email** - Ensure management of your inbox doesn't expose you to the bad brain habit of multitasking by establishing an email schedule. Create a routine of when you will read and act on your emails each day; this could be two, three, or four times a day, perhaps early morning, early afternoon, and a few minutes before business close. Once you create that routine, stick to it. Don't be tempted to review emails outside of your designated times.

When establishing your email routine, think through the ramifications of checking your emails first thing in the morning. By checking email in the morning, are you allowing email to dictate the rest of your day, instead of deciding for yourself what your most important tasks will be for that day?

If you move to a twice daily routine, you may wish to create an automatic response to let your clients, suppliers, co-workers, and boss know. Don't ask to implement a less-frequent email routine, just do it—beg for forgiveness (although unlikely to be needed), don't ask for permission.

In a case study, an employee drowning in emails due to lack of management created a ritual of checking his email just twice a day, at 10.15 am and 2.30 pm. Whereas previously he couldn't keep up with all his messages, he discovered he could clear his inbox each time he opened it—the reward of fully focusing his attention on email for forty-five minutes at a time. He also reset the expectations of all the people he regularly communicated with by email. "I've told them if it's an emergency and they need an instant response, they can call me and I'll always pick up," he said. Nine months later, he had yet to receive such a call!

There is also a health-related reason for scheduling email checks. When University of California Irvine researchers conducted an experiment to measure the heart rates of employees with and without continual access to office email, they discovered something very interesting. Those individuals who received a steady stream of messages stayed in a perpetual "high alert" mode, with correspondingly higher heart rates. Employees without constant email access did less multitasking, and were less stressed because of it!

- **Process messages quickly** - When you open your inbox, process it until you're done. Don't just look at an email and leave it sitting in your inbox. Never put anything in a holding pattern, email or otherwise, if you can avoid it; that's a huge time-waster. Remember OHIO, only handle it once. Don't save an email or a phone call to deal with later. As soon as something gets your attention, you should act on it.

Make it a rule to not leave the inbox with emails hanging around. Work your way from top to bottom, one email at a time. Open each message and take care of it immediately. Remember the four Ds – **Delete, Do, Delegate or Defer.** Your choices:

- **No action required -**
  - o **Delete** - Be brutal. Keep in mind that if you move email messages to the trash bin, this doesn't instantly wipe them out. Later in the day, if you realise you need a deleted message, you can still retrieve it, if you've not yet emptied the trash bin.
  - o **Archive** - If you need to keep a message for later reference, archive it.
- **Do it** - If it requires two minutes or less just do it - act or reply immediately, then archive or delete.
- **Delegate it** – if someone else is the best person to action the email then forward the email, then archive or delete
- **Defer/schedule it** - Put more time-consuming items on your to-do list. Click and drag the email to the calendar, or to your tasks.

Get in and out of the inbox quickly, moving on to the next email. If you practice this enough, you can plough through pages of emails very quickly.

- **If you want to receive less email, send fewer emails -** It's that simple.
- **Be precise, the shorter the email, the better** - When you write an email, say exactly what you mean; use concise, clear, straightforward language and use as few words as possible. Shorter emails get faster responses. Precision also makes it less likely you'll receive subsequent emails generating confusion. Avoid communicating in ways that

lead to lots of follow-up questions, seeking clarity you failed to provide the first time.

- **Be clear on the objective of the email in the subject line and email opener** - The subject line often determines whether an email is opened or not. Ensure the subject line is short and clear and provides details of the email purpose. The subject line or email opener should state whether the email is a request for an action to be taken (and stated deadline) or if it is for information only.

- **Create rules to move specified emails automatically to subfolders or trash** - You can establish rules to automatically move emails from/to a certain person or move a subject containing particular words to a specified subfolder. This is useful for all types of emails such as regular reports you want to retain or group emails that you can't unsubscribe to, but want to automatically delete. A favourite of mine is the meeting acceptance email rule. Most of us don't need to know if someone has accepted (if we occasionally need to know, we can take a look)— only if they have declined or marked the acceptance as tentative. You can set up a rule so that all acceptances automatically go into a certain folder, potentially the trash folder. If you organise a lot of meetings, creation of this rule will reduce the volume of emails significantly.

- **To Cc or not Cc?** - Use the To: and Cc: fields to separate individuals in terms of: who the email message is sent to, denoting that you expect a response from this person or persons, and who is getting the message as a copy only and hence no action or response is required.

Typically, you will receive back two to three times the number of emails you send. The email proliferation occurs largely because of copying others on your original messages.

Cc-ing, however, certainly has a purpose. The reasons you may copy others on an email are: you were asked to, the message provides relevant information for those receiving it, or recipients may need to review the information and take appropriate action in some manner.

However, keep in mind that other motives might prompt you to copy recipients unnecessarily. For example, you might copy your manager because you want him or her to know you've followed through on certain tasks. You are sending your communication as proof of your work, which you might not really need to do. Also, it can be tempting to cc a recipient or two simply because it's the normal culture of this type of communication.

As you begin to reflect on your approach when you copy others on emails, you will likely start to pay attention to your own habits and patterns of cc-ing. You will find that you can streamline your communication methods to cc less and make better use of your time—and even more so of those receiving the emails. Awareness is necessary to save time and energy regarding any work-related task.

- **Use 'reply to all' sparingly** - When you write a reply to an email, remember that you should reply only to recipients who will be directly affected by your communication in the response. This will reduce email traffic and improve communication flow all-round.
- **Unsubscribe from unwanted emails** - Be ruthless in unsubscribing. These emails take up a lot of space in

your inbox over time, not to mention the wasted effort in deleting them each time they come through.

- **Use groups** - If you mail the same group of people repeatedly, set up a group or email alias. In Outlook, it's called a Distribution List. You can save yourself time by not having to type each person's name when you mail the group each and every time.

- **Acknowledge receipt where relevant** - Where relevant, but only where relevant, provide a response to the sender. This lets the sender know you received the message, that you don't require any additional information or context, and therefore, they can check the correspondence off their list. Your response should be short; the fewer words, the better; e.g. "Thanks," "Got it," "Makes sense," etc.

- **Have one calendar** - Have one calendar for all of your appointments in all areas of your life. By doing this, you make it impossible to double-book yourself, and it makes your life simpler.

- **Pick up the phone and make a call, but also know when face-to-face communication is necessary** - When you receive an email with a question that you sense will need a few back and forth messages, pick up the phone or meet face-to-face instead; this may save significant time. In the article "5 Reasons Why Meeting Face-to-Face Is Best," Craig Jarrow explains the benefits of being able to actually see the colleague you're speaking with. He says that meeting in person gives you the opportunity to perceive and interpret the other person's body language. This includes the individual's facial expressions and posture. It's also true that any type of email exchange might go back and forth several times, and the underlying issue at hand may never be clearly identified. If you're actually having a face-to-face with a colleague, you can see this person react and respond. You can deal with problems in real time and avoid infinite email exchange, which permits you to get right to the centre of any problems at hand.

Of course, not all of these inbox management strategies will work for everyone. Clearly, in some roles, you will have to check emails on a regular basis, especially if your business uses email as its main communication tool. No matter what strategies you deploy, remain focused on reducing the time you spend in your inbox.

Check Point:

- ✓ **How much time are you spending managing your inbox?**
- ✓ **Do you need to check emails as often as you do? What focus price are you paying?**
- ✓ **What strategies can you implement to reduce the time spent on managing your emails?**

14

The Well-Run Meeting

Meetings are one of the most significant time investments that organisations make. When you consider the hourly rate of everyone attending, meetings are expensive. You may need to get management approval for a $500 expense, but you can call a one-hour meeting with twenty people and no one notices!

It is the responsibility of leaders to manage the cost of meetings like they would manage other company expenditure. Are you or your leaders shirking this responsibility?

You may have heard sayings such as:

- **A meeting consists of a group of people who have little to say—until after the meeting. (Pamela Shaw)**
- **The least productive people are usually the ones who are most in favour of holding meetings. (Thomas Sowell)**
- **A meeting is an event at which the minutes are kept and the hours are lost. (Joseph Stilwell)**

Meetings do have a place in every organisation. With the right level of attendance, frequency of meetings, pre-work before each one, management in the meeting and post, they are an effective tool. If any of these factors are missing, the meeting will get in the way of real productivity and the organisation's bottom line.

Below are some tips on how to make meetings effective, rather than a productivity killer:

- Be very clear about the purpose/objective. Do you want a decision? Do you want to generate ideas? Is the meeting a status update? Are you communicating something, etc.?
- Does the meeting need to happen? If the anticipated meeting outcomes sound weak, you probably don't need to have the meeting in the first place.
- Should you trim attendance? It is likely that the higher the number of people attending, the less effective the meeting. Consider and reconsider each person invited.
- Set an agenda and ensure it is communicated prior to the meeting.
- Start the meeting on time.
- Stick to the agenda. Redirect discussion to the relevant points, manage ramblers respectfully but firmly, and ensure that the meeting outcomes are met.
- How long does the meeting need to take? Could the meeting be wrapped up in half the time? A short meeting is a good meeting. Short meetings mean everyone remains attentive and forces everyone to get to the point quickly.
- At the end of the meeting, ensure you have agreement. For example, who will do what and by when?
- If the meeting is scheduled longer than ninety minutes, consider a break mid-meeting to ensure focus remains for the duration of the meeting.
- End on time.
- Take accurate minutes. Document and share the main points.

- Question the necessity of recurring meetings. Too often, weekly or monthly meetings are held simply because they are already on everyone's calendar. Periodically, audit recurring meetings to assess whether or not they should continue as is, be restructured and repurposed, or be removed from your schedule completely. Just because a meeting has occurred in the past does not mean it should continue indefinitely.

A number of companies are taking a different approach to meetings to win back some time in their working day. One company only has meetings one day a week—mad meeting Mondays! On Mondays, they ask everyone to come into the office, meet, discuss, and make decisions. The rest of the week is meeting free, allowing greater flexibility of hours and place of work.

Only having meetings one day a week may appear to be too radical a shift for your organisation. A more realistic schedule may be banning meetings on one day of the week: the "meeting fast." This is something that you as an individual can schedule, even if it isn't necessarily sanctioned company-wide. Why not block your diary (not allowing any meetings) one day of the week? The productivity benefits will be immediate.

Check Point:

- ✓ **How can you improve the effectiveness of meetings using the tips above?**
- ✓ **How can you reduce the time you or your team spend in meetings? What action can you take today?**
- ✓ **Could you or your company have at least one day of the week as a "meeting fast"?**

15

Embracing Good Stress

It's difficult to be productive when you're stressed out. It's hard to stay focused because you're thinking about deadlines, problems, or an overwhelming amount of work that needs to be done in what never seems to be enough time.

Stress is a physiological response to a change in our environment, and is designed primarily to keep us safe. It's well documented that stress is at the root of many modern-day ailments, and the workplace remains a key cause of stress. Stress is seen as the primary culprit for all feelings of discomfort and dismay, and to be avoided at all costs. However, whether we like it or not, stress is an unavoidable fact of life.

One of the recent theories regarding stress provides this argument: we basically have stress, not for survival in the immediate sense, but because we wouldn't have the opportunity to learn from the stressful situation without the stress it brings. Early man may have had a stressful reaction so he could escape a tiger, but feeling this kind of pressure is not a healthy way to respond to our lives today. We all need to understand that stress triggers all sorts of mechanisms biologically, and we can learn how to grow and develop psychologically from the pressure. How we react to stress, those times when our heart is pounding, is key to keeping ourselves mentally and physically healthier.

Psychologists say it's not the amount of stress or the severity of it that will harm us. It is actually our belief in whether or not that stress will cause us to sustain harm that matters – the power of our belief!

Rather than believe that stress is toxic, perhaps the key is unlocking what we believe about stress and finding ways to embrace it and use it for good in our lives. If each of us can comprehend that stress has the ability to enhance our performance in life and assist us in personal growth, then it will accomplish that in our lives. We can think of it as a gift, if it's managed properly.

Research tells us that short-term stress can actually improve our immunity. As the body responds to stress at a given time, it is actually preparing one's system for the possibility of some type of infection or injury. A Stanford study conducted in 2012 concluded that lab rats had a clear reaction to mild stress. The rats had a "massive mobilisation" of several different types of immune cells in their blood upon subjection to stress.

Interestingly enough, stress can cause you to become more resilient. When you learn to deal with all types of stressful situations, this can help you deal more easily with stressful situations in the future. This conclusion was reached in a body of research conducted to examine the science of resilience.

Stress can also motivate you to succeed. Good stress may be just the thing you need to get a task completed at your workplace. Consider an impending deadline. Stress can influence your behaviour in a positive way; it can prompt you to manage a situation productively and rapidly. The key is to look at stressful situations as attainable challenges. Tell yourself you can meet it head on, rather than perceiving it as being too overwhelming, an unpassable roadblock.

If you expect to experience stress and fully recognise that you have the natural ability to thrive under pressure, you will be healthier than if you try to avoid all stress by fearing it or suppressing it. Studies show that people who see their racing heart or sweaty palms as a signal that they are receiving energy from the body will actually do better under the stress. They rise to the occasion by performing better than they normally would. In this frame of mind, they make better decisions and end up impressing others with their overall performance in the stressful situation.

There are many ways to approach stress management. The most commonly perceived method is to learn to thrive under pressure, to embrace (and even love) deadlines. It helps to enjoy competition—making up your mind that you always want to push yourself. This type of behaviour and attitude exemplifies the Iron Man model of stress.

However, this approach is just one way of managing stress well. Even if you're not really the type of person who thrives under pressure, and you don't enjoy being competitive, this doesn't mean that you can't learn to be good at handling stress. You may thrive in stressful circumstances in a different way. For instance, you might do this through connection and compassion, not through a sense of competition or feeling aggression. You might have the ability to use stress as a catalyst for connecting with other people—through having compassion, experiencing empathy, and feeling more connection, thereby strengthening your relationships.

Another way of being good at stress involves giving it some type of meaning. This might come from appreciating yourself more and by recognising your strengths, plus appreciating help provided for stressful situations from your community. You might say, "This is going to do something positive for me and other people, so the stress is worth it." Or, you might tell yourself, "Even though I am terrified right now, this experience has helped me cultivate courage." You might also have the ability to look back at a stressful situation and say, "Well, even though this stress was horrible and I wish it hadn't happened, I can take it as a learning experience that gave me knowledge of XYZ." You can deal well with stress by having a philosophical approach, even if you don't run on adrenaline surges or cope by isolating yourself from others during stress.

To manage all aspects of your stress levels and separate good from bad symptoms, keep a positive attitude. Remain calm, even in the face of chaos; assess your options, then decide on the next steps to take; lead others by example; and stay off the drama train. Keep things in perspective, too. Ask yourself this question: What is the very worst thing that could happen, and what is the chance that it actually could happen?

Check Point:

    ✓ **How do you react to stress today?**
    ✓ **Do you recognise your triggers for stress?**
    ✓ **How can you embrace stress?**

16

Make Getting Home For Dinner A Priority

Staying late to meet a deadline or deliver a product on time will occasionally be necessary, but for many, working overtime is the accepted norm and an unhealthy habit. There are a number of reasons for overtime:

- It's required, just to keep up with the amount of work that has to be done.
- Company culture (or perceived culture) supports the idea that those who work longer hours will be promoted more quickly for working "harder."
- Workers want to mimic the hours of a manager. Many managers arrive at the office earlier and depart later than others each day. Their employees may mimic their schedule, because they believe working longer hours is necessary to gain approval.
- The manager expects their team to work longer hours to demonstrate commitment.

Loads of research has proven beyond a doubt that excessive, routine overtime does not, in and of itself, increase productivity. The small bump in extra output you might achieve by staying later is often more than offset by your decreased energy and resultant effectiveness for the rest of the week.

Whether you are working overtime regularly just to keep up with the workload, or due to the other cultural reasons noted above, you can change. Think about how your life would change if you could pick your children up from school one day a week or more, make that exercise class with friends, time on a passion project or simply be home to have dinner with your family or friends.

The productivity tips and tools in the book will allow you to improve your output, helping you get the work done. This alone will not make all the difference, however. You need to believe that it is more than okay to leave the office on time or even early, and make the conscious choice to honour what is truly important to you. You can have it all!

If the Chief Executive Officer of Intel or Chief Operating Officer of Facebook can avoid overtime, you can too.

In his book, *High Output Management*, the late Andy Grove described how in his days as CEO of Intel he always arrived to work by eight in the morning, but never left later than six—and never took work home with him! Despite all the challenges of leading a giant, fast-growing tech company, Grove says he always kept a schedule that allowed him to be home for dinner. Grove explains his scheduling secret this way: "My day ends when I'm tired and ready to go home, not when I'm done. I am never done. Like a housewife's, a manager's work is never done. There is always more to be done, more that should be done, always more than can be done."

Facebook Chief Operating Officer Sheryl Sandberg explains her finish to each working day: "I walk out of the office every day at 5.30 pm so I'm home for dinner with my kids at six, and interestingly, I've been doing that since I had kids." She goes on to say, "I did that when I was at Google, I do it at Facebook, but I would say it's not until the last two years that I'm brave enough to talk about it publicly. I certainly wasn't running around giving speeches on it."

To make up for leaving work at 5.30 pm, Sandberg said early on she would send emails to her colleagues during late hours at night and very early in the morning. This served as proof she was still totally committed to her work. She says, "I was showing everyone I worked just as hard. I was getting up earlier to make sure they saw my emails at 5.30 am, staying up later to make sure they saw my emails late. But now I'm much more confident in where I am and so I'm able to say, 'Hey! I am leaving work at 5.30.' And I say it very publicly, both internally and externally." Sandberg is sending a much-needed message that it's okay to leave work before dark.

Having overly full schedules for both parents and children, does make it difficult to actually have family dinners. But, if you become aware of the benefits from regularly eating together at the table, you may try harder to do so.

Research points to the fact that having dinner together as a family a minimum of four times a week has positive effects on child development and well-being.

In 2010, a study was published entitled, "The Importance of Family Dinners," by Columbia University's National Center on Addiction and Substance Abuse. Researchers found that teenagers who actually sat down to enjoy dinner with their families, regularly, were better students. They were twice as likely to receive grades in school within the A and B range. In addition, these students were three times more likely to say they had a great relationship with their parents. These same teenagers also had fewer experiences with substance abuse, and were documented to be less prone to experiencing any type of eating disorder.

In a New Zealand study, a higher frequency of eating meals with their families was strongly associated with positive moods in teenagers. Similarly, other researchers have concluded that teenagers who dine with their families on a regular basis also enjoy a more positive view of the future, compared to their peers who don't eat with their parents.

Furthermore, research shows that conversation at the dinner table enhances vocabulary for young children, even more so than having adults read aloud to them. The researchers documented the number of rare words (those not on a list of the 3,000 most commonly used words) that were used by families while talking at dinner. It was documented that young children learned 1,000 rare words having dinner with their families, compared to only 143 rare words learned from parents reading aloud.

Backed up by over twenty years of research, these benefits are shared by Anne K. Fishel, PhD, co-founder of The Family Dinner Project. A professor at Harvard Medical School, she is the author of *Home for Dinner*, in which she notes that it benefits the brain, body and spirit when individuals sit down with family for a nightly meal.

Challenging your working hours will not only benefit your own effectiveness but also has significant benefits for your family. Whether it be the well-being of your family, or equally important, your own well-being, prioritise getting home for dinner as if it was a 6 pm meeting with your most important client: not to be missed!

Check Point:

- ✓ **What is keeping you in the office that prevents you from having dinner with your family or friends?**
- ✓ **What needs to change, so that you can be home for dinner?**
- ✓ **What action can you take toward leaving work on time today?**

17

Introduction To Interviews

I've had the opportunity to interview the CEOs or partners of some great Australian and global companies from retail to financial services, professional services and recruitment. They all offer different perspectives on managing life-work balance, challenges, flexibility, and productivity opportunities. Each one has provided some great tips and techniques for success.

Enjoy the read.

18

Interview with Stella Petrou Concha, CEO Reo Group

"When you succeed, I succeed".

Co-founder, CEO and driving force behind the fast-growing brand Reo Group, Stella's mission and purpose is to help others succeed - Stella is personally driven to awaken and positively impact the lives of the people in the Finance profession as a whole.

Initially starting a career in medicine, she quickly realised that the healthcare sector was not her true passion and found a strong alignment in the recruitment industry. Upon discovering her career purpose of elevating human potential, Stella founded Reo in her late twenties, and it is now a BRW Fast 100 company, winning a variety of industry awards. Reo now houses some of Sydney's top finance executives who have strategically made a move from commercial finance into finance recruitment and talent development.

Reo's purpose is elevating human potential by nurturing and developing people to create opportunity.

What is your definition of work-life balance, and how do you manage it?

For me it comes down to having a clear understanding of your values and being connected to your values.

Firstly, I don't have work-life balance. I have work-life integration. What I do well is counterbalance work and life. When life needs me more than work, then I'm there, and when work needs me more than life, I'm there. My life value hierarchy is marriage and family first and foremost. This comprises of my relationship with my spouse; my children; my health; and my relationships with family and friends. I think that if any one of these fails, it has a much deeper impact on my whole life than if work was to fail. I pay much closer attention to my marriage, my children, my health, and my family than I do to work—but that doesn't necessarily mean that it takes up more of my time.

What I also know is this: when I put my needs first (in my case marriage and family), work is amazing. I believe that we're energetic beings, and the results that you get in your life is just a reflection of the person in the mirror. So when you satisfy your needs first, everything tends be in flow.

For me work-life balance is about being connected to my values; my first value is marriage and then the children. Third is my business. What I ask myself every day is: have I given my love, my attention, my intimacy and my joy to my husband and my children? Of a morning, it's a kiss, saying good morning. It's not just walking next to one another in the corridor; it's absolutely being present. It could also breakfast with the kids; so I will start work at 8.30 am or 9 am, so I can have my moment in the morning with the kids. When my husband and my children have a moment with me in the morning, it might only be fifteen minutes; it sets their day up well—which means that the day ends well, not only for them but also for me.

I'm not a late finisher; I'm home by 5.30 pm every day, and I give another three hours to my family at night. Everything in between is work. So, I know that if I'm spending time with my family in the morning and my family at night, that keeps me happy and congruent with my values—and that means that I'm absolutely on fire during the day.

What are your secrets/tips/techniques for success in life balance?

I think that the secret sauce or the secret tip is allocating at least thirty minutes to sixty minutes on yourself every day. That could look like exercise, planning, or self-reflection. What that does is sets up how you need to play your next day. As I just mentioned I believe in work-life counterbalance, so a counterbalance might mean you put your energy into one thing more than the other, depending on what needs you more. If the kids are sick, I'm at home; if I need to deliver on a project, I'm on at work. It's a counterbalance, so spending at least an hour on yourself every day allows you to stay connected to what needs to have more of your attention in the next moment of life.

I think that consistently staying connected to who I am is crucial. I spend at least an hour every morning on that; it's a habit.

It's funny—put yourself first and the rest will follow.

What do you consider some of the greatest challenges that employees working in an office environment face today?

I have built my whole business around this so I'm passionate about this question. Reo's biggest challenge is helping our clients attract and retain talent. We work with some of the best companies out there and they want the best, but they can't retain the best, because they don't deliver the best leadership.

Every company has its issues with systems; profits; market presence etc. These conversations have been happening for a long time, but that's not the conversation that we should be having. The conversation that we should be having is: what are we doing to consistently elevate our people? We need to shift the focus from cost / profit to people. That's it; if we can do that, people will stay in organisations, organisations will retain their staff, and businesses will perform better.

Businesses are nothing without their people; the people are just energy vortexes. I'm a ball of energy, you're a ball of energy, and we interact. If my energy is open and positive, you're going to feel great around me. But if my energy is closed, sad, angry, frustrated, and stressed, you will feel exactly what I'm feeling. That's what we're seeing out there in the market place. A soup pot of negative emotions.

The brain uses the limbic system to set our emotions. The limbic system seeks information from the outside world to tell it what to feel. My emotional centre will look at you, make a snap judgement and tell me how I should feel about you. It will tell me that you are either good or you are a threat. The answer that I get will depend on how I judge you, perceive you, and feel towards you. This is a really good system as it's our primitive fight or flight response. It is great for crossing the road, understanding when the baby's nappy needs to be changed. However, it is bad in business if we don't learn how to use our emotional centres. Not all companies are talking about this. A handful of companies teach their people emotional intelligence or emotional control. This needs to come to the forefront of all leadership conversations. When we l know how to control our own emotions and how our emotions affect others, then businesses can operate harmoniously and they can elevate to the next level.

When we do this as a cohort of leaders, we won't hold our people in at work until ten o'clock at night, because we know how impactful that is on all the centres of their life—from their marriage, children, sleep cycles, to their physical well-being. When you deplete all those other centres, it will bring work down.

So, it's foolish, what we are doing today. The more companies do it, the more they fail; and you see it.

Do you think emotional intelligence is something that comes more naturally to some of us than others?

I believe the evolution of the individual and their awareness of their self reflects as emotional intelligence. It can be learnt. However, it takes time to learn it, so it needs to start in school and continue in university. It needs to be fostered by parents. And it certainly needs to be a conversation at every level of the development of the candidate that's sitting in an organization.

How do you manage your communication, including your inbox, ensuring you have the right balance between effective communication and management of your time? Is email management a challenge for you?

Email management is not a challenge for me because I have a personal rule: if you want to communicate with me, talk to me. An email is just confirmation of what's been communicated, it's not a form of communication.

We've got a rule in Reo: limited communication over email. That's for candidates and clients. We are a call centre so we don't measure emails. We are interested in how many connections are made over the phone or in person. Emails don't sign contracts. Deep relationships led by conversation build business. Emails don't get you a job; an interview gets you a job. We do not use emails to communicate; we only use an email to clarify a point or come back to a conversation that we want a confirmation of.

The other issue similar to emails is voice messages. I never listen to my voice messages in a timely manner—but I do respond to text messages. My voice message recording articulates, "Sorry you haven't been able to contact me; if your message is urgent, please text me." There are some poor habits where people pass a monkey by leaving a voice message. Recently I deleted Facebook off my phone, because people thought that because they were commenting on my posts or my pictures and sending me messenger emails that I was receiving them, but I wasn't.

Bottom line for me is that if you haven't spoken, it's not communicated.

What are some of your habits and routines that are key to your life balance and success?

I have lots of habits and routines because I have two kids under the age of four and an executive role requiring full time hours. My first habit is at the beginning of the day. I wake up at 6 am and either exercise or meditate. I'll then have breakfast with my kids. If I can't exercise in the morning I will go at lunch. I exercise four days a week.

I always plan the night before, so I have a plan ready to go in the morning. I apply the rule of 'the first four hours a day are the most productive and the most important,' because it's when you have your most energy and your most focus. I only do the one thing that is the most important thing for me that day, which will make everything else in my day easy and in flow.

I don't consider myself a morning or night person. I've been trained as a salesperson and I know from the last fifteen years, the important gets done in the morning. Admin, socialization gets done in the afternoon.

The brain's ability to metabolize energy peaks is in the morning. This is science. For people that chew their morning up, my question to them would be: Is that because you're clouded on your vision? If you are clear on your purpose for the day, you can probably start your morning on point. If you are trying to get through the greyness of who you are and what your purpose is in life every single day, that probably takes up the first part of your day.

The end of my day is planning. I always plan at the end of the day. I wrap up my day by planning for the following day and it also includes a conversation with my husband. I tie off everything about Reo at the end of the day and then I go home and become Mum. I put my jammies on, take the jewellery off, start cooking, and feed and bathe the kids. I'm busy. I have very little time for anything else but my health, my work, my children, and my family. About 8.30 pm I usually sit on the lounge with a book to read, and that's usually a self-development book or some sort of leadership book, and I write notes and reflect on my day, talk to my husband, have a cup of coffee, and then crash.

I have some bad habits too, mainly around eating; I'll eat when I'm bored. I'll have a very healthy week, and then I've got some real weaknesses around self-control on the weekend. Another bad habit is wasting time with social media. Sometimes, I'll click on to Instagram and see what's going on. It's like I've missed out on three hours of my life, but I only have thirty minutes left in my day to connect with my husband.

What are your thoughts on flexibility within the workforce, including flexible hours and working from home?

I believe in full flexibility and trust. I also believe people can operate as they chose so long as you have provided them a framework that helps being out the best in your team.

Our vision at Reo is to elevate human potential. We are just about to roll out a "me day" which is a monthly rostered day off to recharge and repair. This will give our team an additional two weeks leave per year. The corporate life style is not a nine to five work expectation. People work at night and on weekends. You have to give them the flexibility during the week to pace themselves so they don't burn out.

What would the perfect working week look like for you, if you were designing it today?

I would design it differently. The first thing that I would do is make it project-oriented. So, people could strive to achieve, because we are hunters and gatherers at the end of the day. The other thing that I would do is spend time to reflect on yourself. The key thing for me is that every single individual needs to be working on their own evolution as a consciousness—and only in that instance can they work little or long hours, depending on what they need to do.

Working on yourself can come in different forms. The purpose of this is to bring mindfulness and presence into the now. It could be physical exercise; it may be reading personal development book, or taking a course; being involved in something other than your day-to-day work. Do something that challenges the evolution of the mind to think and be different every single day. If you've got people that are consistently evolving and being creative, they will have capacity to think beyond the norm. This will bring joy and wellness to the individual making for a more productive work week.

What are the areas of opportunity in the productivity arena that you routinely witness and experience?

There are a few models out there. There are two that I work with. The first is being effective. Being effective is doing the right thing at the right time. For me it's doing the right things at the beginning of the day I can only do this through effective planning.

The other model that I use is the Eisenhower model, doing things that are important but not urgent are the items that are going to propel you forward. That is when you are in your zone and working on elevation. As a leader, you should be spending 20 percent of your time in this quadrant. Anything that's urgent and important, (doing of your job) is when you're in demand and there is a time pressure. It's hard for leaders to get out of this space.

Poor use of time is operating in the "urgent and not important" box. An example of this is responding to an email when an email comes in. The "not urgent and not important" box for me is wasting time flicking through social media icons. I call this a distraction.

If you can self-reflect and be brutally honest with yourself and know what percentage of your time goes into distractive and not important items, you will get an idea of what you need to do to be productive. You can self-analyse and get rid of as many distractions as you can and replace them with more productive habits.

What are your top tips or takeaways for success?

The first one is counterbalance work and home. Accordingly, when one needs you more than the other, go with the flow.

Secondly, acknowledge that you need work more than work needs you. Work can find another "you" a dozen times a day. You need work to grow. You need to give work the best of you, and what work should give you is an environment for growth and prosperity. Most educated professionals grow in a work environment. If you are not growing, perhaps it's an opportunity to ask to be involved in a project or perhaps it's time to seek new employment.

The next big tip is honour your values. Never let your highest priorities and values to fall by the wayside. Not prioritising high values such as family or health can cause a great destruction in all areas of your life. If you drop the ball on work, it can bounce back. If you drop the ball on your health, it's not as easy to bounce back. If you drop the ball on spending time with family and nurturing your kids, you can't really bounce out of that. Disease and divorce are not events we really plan for in life.

The fourth tip is prioritise your self-elevation and your self-leadership because that will draw inspiration for your people to become a better version of yourself.

And my final is to acknowledge that you are a ball of energy. People can feel what you're feeling through the limbic open-loop emotional system. Work as hard as you can to be in a positive vibrational state. Do whatever you can to keep yourself resonating with love and joy, because when you resonate with that, people will resonate with you. That's how you become a leader. That's how you can positively change humanity. That's how you can positively grow your career, because people will want to promote you because you're awesome to work with. That's how you can be in the space of creativity because you're not thinking with fear, you're thinking with opportunity. Greatness comes out of all those emotions, so work as hard as you can to stay in a positive emotional vibrational state.

19

Interview with Guy Russo, CEO Wesfarmers Limited Department Stores Division (Kmart and Target Australia Limited)

Guy joined Wesfarmers Limited in 2008 as Managing Director of Kmart Australia (including Kmart Tyre and Auto Service). He was appointed Chief Executive Officer of their Department Stores division, which along with Kmart also incorporates Target Australia, in February 2016. Prior to this, Guy worked for McDonald's, beginning his career in 1974. He was appointed Managing Director and Chief Executive Officer at McDonald's Australia in 1999 before

becoming President, McDonald's Greater China from 2005 to 2007. He is currently on the Board of Guzman y Gomez and is President of One Sky Foundation.

What is your definition of work-life balance, and how do you manage it?

Most people talk to how you manage your work time versus your personal family time. I've added another piece into this where I communicate with my team members about work time, family time, and also me time.

A lot of people think about work and life balance as being when you're at work, it's work time and when you're at home, it's home time. However, there is a lot of crossover that happens in the daytime that might be required for family time. My example is that you've got a Monday to Friday job and the kids have got something on at school in the morning, or they've got something at school during the daytime. The working partner(s) needs to find an opportunity to make sure that they can be present for their children as well as their work. So, my view is that the day and night is not as black and white as people seem to think. When I was first CEO at McDonald's, I wanted to do canteen duty at my children's school during the workday or reading groups for the kids at school. So, I just made sure that fitted in. I've given the example of children at school, but it may not be children—it may be other family, health or other things that happen from time to time.

In the workforce, there needs to be flexibility to slot in those critical family or other times during the daytime, and the reverse happens when you're at home with work things going on, whether it's receiving emails, texts, etc. I'm not suggesting taking work home, but a lot of people see this is as black and white, day and night, work versus family time—but in today's environment, I think we all need to be a lot more flexible around how this works.

I find that you can't write up policies for a lot of these requirements. When the workplace changes, the immediate reaction is to start writing some policies, and I think the more policies we write, the more rules are created and the more rigid we become. We need guidelines, but we need to have a flexible environment, which will benefit both the worker and the organisation.

There are some things that you should plan; and the way I command my balance is around November each year, I normally plan the whole year out. I plot into the diary for the whole year everything to do with the family, and the children, and my life. So, putting in holidays, anniversaries, putting in school events to ensure they are a priority before the work schedule starts filling. So, diarise your personal life as much you do your work life, so there's a bigger chance of both happening.

In relation to me time, that's something I've just thought about more so in the last twelve months when I've taken this new role overseeing Kmart, Kmart Auto, and being hands on with Target. It's probably something I should have given thought to throughout my career. I think one way that you can energise yourself is to be a little more selfish for your own personal time. I spend a lot of time on planes, in hotels, so I normally try to get some personal time then to re-energise, and this helps me be a better employee, parent and partner. A lot of people think when you're at work, you've got to be there for your team, and when you're home, you're there for the family, but don't think about me time. Having time to yourself allows you to re-energise, so you have the energy for everyone that's in your life, both at work and at home. Your health also goes into that, scheduling health check-ups. An assessment of your individual health is as important an assessment as your work assessment—to ensure you can prevent health issues and/or improve your quality of life.

What do you consider some of the greatest challenges that employees face today?

When I think of challenges, I start with what the business outcomes are meant to be and what are the resulting challenges for individuals. With Target and Kmart, the major outcome required as a business is profitable returns to shareholders. And when you know what your major goal is at work, or why are you coming to work, you can then distil that into your team—to make sure that whatever challenges they have, that firstly you set specific goals about why they're there.

So, for myself and my team, we're here for commercial reasons; but importantly, those commercial outcomes need to be achieved in the right way: having great values. So, you start with what your purpose is in business and then what are the objectives of the team to achieve that purpose. To achieve the desired outcome, you need to understand who the company is. When I joined Kmart and Target, both companies needed to more clearly define what their purpose was.

Once the company's purpose is clear, the commercial outcomes are known and the values are understood, the next step is for teams to be clear on what they need to do in their space to deliver on those outcomes. If you don't clearly define what is your purpose, outcomes, and what business you're in, a lot of team members get caught up in the spinning wheel of coming to work and not a great sense of achievement.

The aim is to work in an organisation that is running smoothly; it's delivering outcomes to shareholders and the workplace is fun and friendly. I've visited a few of those over the last ten years; so, I think of Uber, I think of Google, and I think of Apple. They have clarity of purpose, really focused on shareholder outcomes and the environment is really humming; team members just look so relaxed and so focused on delivering. The reverse happens in an environment where pressure or challenge is in work environments. When those things aren't in place, you normally find that you've got chaos. Back in the early days, in Kmart's case, a lot of team members were ducking for cover; there was talk of whether the business would be sold, and they were just worried about whether there was going to be a future or not.

How do you manage your communication, including your inbox, ensuring you have the right balance between effective communication and management of your time?

I can't emphasise enough the importance of communication. I have a phrase about being on the field and being present. In my role, I have responsibilities for close to 800 stores—that's in Australia and New Zealand—and on top of those 48,000 team members there are close to 2,000 team members working out of support offices for Target, Kmart, and Kmart Auto. And then there are teams in India, Bangladesh, Hong Kong, and China so communication for me is absolutely mission critical.

The best style of communication is being present, being in front of the team. So, while I can't be in front of the entire work force, which is around 50,000 team members, I can make my way around Australia and New Zealand and bring together the leaders of the stores, the store managers. I meet with them about twice a year, talking about the things we referred to before: commercial outcomes, values, and delivering on that promise to yourself and shareholders. So, physical presence is the best way to motivate and guide a workforce. At least twice a year I will also travel to Bangladesh, Shanghai, Hong Kong, and India. Mine and my leadership team's role is to ignite the passion in our team members in Australia, New Zealand and around the world and encourage their commitment to the success of our businesses.

Aside from communication when physically present, email is the obvious means of communication. The teams love to hear from the leader about what's working, what's not working, and how we're doing. The other tool I've engaged with probably more so over the last five years is Facebook. I use my personal Facebook page to communicate to all stakeholders. I'm conscious that it's also my family Facebook page, so I'm exposing my personal life to the team, which I don't worry about so much because the reality is we've all got two lives, work life and personal life, and what I'm trying to do with Facebook is say that who I am on the field and off the field is the same person.

The other form of communication I've used more frequently in the last twelve months is WhatsApp, which is another form of communication that is outstanding; you can get instant messaging. It's especially useful for the stores for what's happening and instant communication from the field about what they're seeing. This may be communicating good or bad news, or sometimes it's just providing input on customers, which provides feedback on whether our strategies are working. Sometimes, the team will just take a picture of somebody in the tea room who's celebrating forty years with the company, letting us know. They are too far away for me to physically visit, but I can pick up the phone and congratulate them on their fortieth year.

So, communication is mission critical. I believe that if you're not on the field and you're not engaging, whether being present or using technology, the team is second-guessing on what the leader is thinking, and feeling. I'm a big fan of communication. I don't think you can overdo it.

What are some of your habits and routines that are key to your life balance and success?

I get up early in the morning. I normally wake up about 5 am and then I'm normally in bed about 10 pm. So, I normally get about seven hours' good sleep, and I always feel refreshed when I get up at five. The 5 am wake-up normally starts with me sitting down, having a cup of coffee and just pondering the day, and maybe reflecting a little on the night before—but that's not an unusual habit.

I'm not sure if it's a habit, but I love going home. I think it's important in life to be happy. I treasure going home to my family. So, at the moment there's a lot on with the Target business, and the team are conscious about trying to fix the business. So, being in love with whomever is at home—for me it's my wife Deanne and the three kids—is important. The habit of wanting to go home each night helps my day.

During the day, I have lots of meetings in my diary, whether that be board meetings with the parent company, board meetings for Kmart and Target, team meetings, and meetings around financial results, to name a few. My habit is to leave as much time in my diary free as I can, so I can get up and walk the floor or walk the shop floor, without being handcuffed and stuck in a room going from meeting to meeting. So, I'd say my strongest work habit is leaving the diary as free as possible to be able to have engagement with the team in the stores, or the teams in the offices, or the teams in Asia.

All offices have lunch rooms, and of course all the stores have lunch rooms as well. When I'm in the office having lunch, I'll make a habit of having it with team members. Again, it allows you to hear what is going on, be on the field, and have a chat to the team about their life outside work. In the stores, the store manager invariably asks: do I want to go to a coffee shop for a coffee? But, I prefer to have a coffee in the tea room. Every time I have a coffee in the tea room, inevitably team members that are serving customers or unloading trucks or filling shelves walk into the tea room, and I can immediately gauge how people are feeling—or people having an opportunity to engage with me about work, or whatever it be, about life.

Another habit is that when I walk into the office of a morning, I make a point of saying hello to the receptionist, the person who has the critical face-to-face contact with anyone visiting the office. And in the stores, it's hard not to say hello to the very first person you see when you walk in the store; this person – the customer greeter, I'll spend a few minutes introducing myself to those people.

My habit at the end of the workday is that as soon as I get home the work gear goes off and I'm into casual gear: out of my work uniform and into my home uniform! This relaxes me immediately when I get home.

What are your thoughts on flexibility within the workforce, including flexible hours and working from home?

I've got a lovely story to share with you. In about 2010 my CFO, Marina, came to me and said she wanted to have a meeting and she told me she was going to have her first child. I was obviously really excited. She also told me she needed to resign or step down as CFO and my reaction was why. As I recall, she said, "I'm not sure how a business of this size with about $4 billion in revenue and 30,000 employees can operate without a CFO." She wanted to have twelve months off, as she was legally entitled to do, and in the second year wanted to consider working from home, so she couldn't commit to what the second year would look like.

My immediate reaction was we will have someone to fill in for the period of her maternity leave and beyond if needed. I couldn't imagine anyone better as my CFO, and her needing to have time off didn't alter my view. She took the twelve months off and then returned three days a week to the office and two days from home. After a year, she added a further day in the office, continuing to work from home for the balance of her week.

Two years after Marina sat down and had the first chat, she came to me again to have a similar chat, pregnant with her second child. Anyway, we're nearly seven years on since that conversation and Marina is now CFO of Kmart, Kmart Auto and Target.

It was only a few days ago, I had a meeting with the real estate department, who reports through to Marina, and the meeting was scheduled from 8 am to midday. The night before the meeting, I got a message from Marina saying, "I know you won't mind, but I won't be in at eight o'clock; Christopher is getting an award at school assembly on Monday morning. I'll see you at ten." That story tells you my whole view of flexibility.

Whether it's at the stores or the office or distribution centres, I expect all managers to sit down with their team members who need flexibility in their life. There is obviously the award (minimum work entitlements), this is another form of a policy, a statutory policy. I think you can go beyond the award and provide the environment that allows for how life is day to day, whether that be someone is not well, children are getting an award at school, someone needing time to train for a triathlon, or taking an extended holiday. You won't find it in an HR policy, but work around it to make it work for everyone.

What are the areas of opportunity in the productivity arena that you routinely witness and experience?

I don't worry about people attending meetings or reading volumes of emails; productive opportunities for me are more in relation to commercial outcomes.

I come from a point of trust, so I trust if someone is in a meeting they need to attend. Re meetings, firstly all meetings are open doors, and if someone thinks they need to know something, then go in—and more importantly, if you don't need to be at that meeting, then don't bother going in. And if you're working from home, have the day off or miss the meeting, just check the minutes or catch up with a colleague when you return re the content of the meeting.

My focus is more from a commercial sense. Kmart sells about 800 million items a year. And if you think about that 800 million items we sell a year, they are all designed from scratch, mostly on a computer—and then the fabric needs to be chosen, colours have to be chosen, and the dimensions and sizing needs to be worked out. It's a very, very complex system that starts at a keyboard, and then that concept needs to be sent to Asia for a sample to be made. The sample needs to be sent back, and then they need to make them; the truck needs to pick them up from the factory, and they need to be shipped. The ship gets to Melbourne, the trucks then deliver to the stores, the stores unload the truck, put the product on the shelf, and then the product is sold through a register.

We have huge amounts of touch points on how our business runs, and huge costs from the design piece to the selling piece. The challenge is, how do you make that simpler? Which is why I don't worry about why someone's got an email, or if he's in the meeting. The bigger priority is finding an efficient way to get from design to sale.

The example I like to use is the Hong Kong rail system. The whole system is underground; it's totally air-conditioned; there are no conductors, no train drivers, no tickets, and they run perfectly. So, when I think of productivity I think about: how do you get the Hong Kong rail system into a system as complex as retail to improve productivity and reduce the costs of moving stuff, and repurpose that spend in other parts of the organisation—customer service as an example?

What are your tips/takeaways for success?

The first one is to get real clarity from your boss about how he or she is going to measure your success at the end of a month, at the end of six months and/or, at the end of twelve months. Know what your goals are.

The second point is: values are so important. I'm not talking about culture at this point. I'm talking about integrity and working with your fellow team members, or managing up and down or sideways and doing that the right way. And if you want to lose your job, do something that is unethical. I normally watch people lose their jobs on the values piece not achieving success from the first point. You could go backwards on your goals, and only after multiple years of poor results, risk your job. If you do something that lacks integrity, then that could lead to instant dismissal.

The third one is from Peter Ritchie. He always stressed the importance of having fun, and I would widen the fun piece to enjoy life whether it be at work or home. I don't see many people who are miserable at home and happy at work that end up being great employees. The best employees that normally surface in any organisation, whether they're at a cash register, unloading a truck, or in the management team in the office—when you do an analysis—normally, they have a great balance between home and work. So, the third one would be fun and enjoyment of life all hours of the day.

Another one is diversity. Diversity is now a very important part of my management style. I think that was the missing link in the '80s and '90s, when I was growing up in my career. It wasn't on my radar, and when I used to hear about it, I didn't get it. So therefore, I used to dismiss it. So, diversity—getting it, understanding it—and more importantly, making sure that you've got a very diverse workforce, a business for everybody.

And lastly, communication. Communication is mission critical, and you can't overdo it.

20

Interview with Katrina Zdrilic, Partner Ernst & Young

Katrina Zdrilic is a working mum of three boys and a Partner at EY (formerly Ernst & Young). She provides financial accounting and assurance services to some of Australia largest and most successful companies.

Katrina joined EY as a graduate over twenty years ago. During her time at EY she has enjoyed many roles, including two years as part of the Technical Consulting group, working on transaction/due diligence projects including IPOs, debt raisings and staplings. Katrina has enjoyed secondments at two of Australia's largest companies as Deputy CFO and CFO to support their finance functions. For a number of years, she was head of the Real Estate assurance group, a team of seventy people serving clients in the real estate sector of Australia, and was responsible for the group's performance.

As part of her role as Partner on audit clients she deals with directors and C-Suite across a range of sectors including retail, consumer products, real estate and media. Katrina is also on the Audit Committee of Macquarie University Hospital.

What is your definition of work-life balance, and how do you manage it?

For me the definition of work-life balance is about effectively integrating each with the other in such a way that I am successfully allocating my efforts and energy in a positive way and achieving the outcomes I want for each. What guides this allocation and integration are my values –which mean me being present, being engaged and connected with family, work and friends. And sometimes this means compromise, that's part of life. There are certain things I won't compromise. For me this means my husband and three sons, they come first, and being there when it really counts, and being present when I am at home, just spending time with them.

I enjoy my work and contribute and gain so much out of it, but home needs me too and I want to be there, so I try to be involved in as much as I can from drop offs, assemblies, homework and assignments, social aspects of school, sport etc. At the same time, I have responsibilities at work and with technology today and phones mean I'm connected with work constantly, so getting home at a reasonable hour, having rules with respect to the phone and doing work from home are important parts of ensuring I get the integration of work-life balance right for me.

On the whole, I feel like I do balance work and life, but certain days the balance doesn't work, and that's usually when the unpredictable happens. In my case, and I think it's probably the case with lots of women, we're good organisers, good project managers, good thinkers and jugglers of all the things that need to be done. So, we put control mechanisms into home life, work life, and social life to manage as much as can be planned. When the little unexpected things happen they're okay, because we've probably got a bit of shock absorption capacity every day—but when lots of little unexpected things happen in one day, or one very big thing happens in one day, that can throw things out the window. And sometimes, whatever control mechanisms are put in place, they will just not work that day.

The feeling of work-life imbalance was probably more common many years ago—when I was the mum of very young children and working my way up through EY with some pretty big hours and some big responsibilities, both at home and at work. At that time of my life, I felt torn in two: torn between my little ones at home and putting in big hours at EY. I often felt like I had to work on my day off; and at times, I found that very difficult, because that was supposed to be my day with my sons.

For me, psychology became important as I got older, more accepting and more understanding that it was an integration of work and life rather than each being separate and never crossing paths in allocated times. When I understood this, and appreciated this was the norm for working women in today's world, especially with more senior roles, then it was like a weight was lifted off my shoulders. I became less hard on myself and more adaptable. I probably became even more focused with my time!

There was a big turning point for us as a family when the boys started school. In the early years, we were very fortunate to have grandparents to help with the kids when I was at work. This gave my husband and I peace of mind that the kids were with family who would give them the love and care we wanted for them when we were at work. So, when they started school, that was a turning point, who was going to pick them up at 3 pm? My husband and I were both in high-pressure jobs. We had to make a choice, which was: will we get a nanny or will we make a work/lifestyle choice? We decided that we wanted one of us to be there for our boys at the end of each school day and all the activities and support they needed, so my husband left where he worked and started working for himself, working from home.

We made this decision for us; it was the right thing for us. We were fortunate, as it seems to have worked out for us. You don't know the circumstances for each family, so my rule is you shouldn't judge anyone for their work/life decisions. And I say that because I've been through pockets where I've been highly judged, like many women who work and have families. But as I said, each family and person needs to work out what works for them.

To make work be as successful as it can and not flow into my family hours, I have become a project manager guru and have organised as much as I can, both in terms of my diary at work around which I have certain rules. These include, gaps in every day, to allow for the unexpected. I start at 9 am most days, which means I can do drop offs. I try to work from home at least five to six days a month. This means I can do school pickups, attend after school activities and get some housework done. I have rules around my phone, which include not looking at emails after a certain time of night and definitely not just before I go to sleep. We have family rules like no phones at meal time. I have outsourced what I can e.g. house cleaning and ironing, so my time at home is with my family.

Tony, my husband, and I have clear roles that we have designated each other around the more administrative parts of running a home and we try to share these. We agreed that on important days in our kids' lives, at least one of us would always be there if not both of us—whether that was a sports carnival, first day at school, parent/teacher interview, or whatever—that was important to us. This has nearly always worked. I wanted to have a level of involvement in the school, which hasn't been as much as I've wanted, but at least two days a year in canteen, so my boys see me there. We agreed what we wanted in our family life, and I think on the whole we've achieved that.

I think personal time is really important as well. And time for just my husband and I. This usually means after dinner, when the kids are asleep, we get to sit down and talk about our days or what's topical. I am not so good at finding personal time, I keep promising myself I will take up yoga but never seem to!

What do you consider some of the greatest challenges that employees face today?

In general, I think the greatest challenges that employees face today is having a job or employer that gives them a sense of purpose or connectivity to their values whilst giving them the balance in their work-life they are seeking. I see more and more today, that the values of an organisation are important to the employees and their engagement and retention. In general, today's younger employees are less sticky to an organisation and seem to move employers frequently to gain experiences/skills. So, this creates pressure on employers to make their work place attractive to retain talent.

I think younger employees are so tech-savvy and seemed to have learnt stop start capabilities that they are able to integrate their work and life more seamlessly through their technology and connectivity. I am amazed at how they can jump between emails, work documents, having conversations and social network fluidly and their brains seem to move from one to the other so smoothly.

Employees can be challenged to stay engaged, motivated or productive if the organisation they work for is one they don't feel connected to. This connection comes from alignment of values, employees feeling they belong and their contribution is valued, they are stretched to reach the next level and are learning. I think for employees – getting the right work-life balance for them can be a challenge. Especially in more recent years when affordability of housing or general affordability in Australia has become an issue.

The biggest challenge we have in audit at EY is retaining talent. The challenge is around people questioning what they want out of their life, and I think that a lot of young people today focus more on what is important to them. And they just don't want to work the long hours which come with the job, especially in certain months of the year.

We are a business that is all about our clients, and so you can put as much control in place as you can but you can't always stop the long hours. If something runs late, then it just runs late and the work needs to get done; the deadline doesn't move. During my twenty-seven years with EY the tolerance to long hours appears to be declining.

What are the areas of opportunity in the productivity arena that you routinely witness and experience?

Businesses expect people to work a certain number of hours; and therefore, there's an expectation that all those hours are productive, but they're not.

I think productivity can be improved everywhere. When you think about the hierarchy of work, most people don't know what people in their team are doing all the time. And, I see this with my clients and in my team. It's only when you starting digging, in a positive way, that you realise that people often fill their days doing things that they don't need to do because they don't know any different.

Technology can assist in improving inefficiency in business processes but first, you need to understand the process and what is the purpose, outcome and benefit of the process. More people need to challenge: is there a better way to do that and does it in fact need to be done at all?

The hours worked should also be questioned. I was once at an organisation that expected people to stay till 7 pm and it was looked upon poorly if an employee didn't, like they weren't carrying their weight. The reality was no one was doing anything productive anyway after 6 pm and were filling in time till 7 pm! It is not how many hours you work but rather what value you have produced.

Looking at myself I spend an hour coming to work, I spend an hour going home, I have elements of unproductiveness because I'm in an open work plan. For me, I personally believe I am way more productive when I'm at home, way more productive in terms of deliverable/churn, getting things done. The down side is

I'm interacting less with my teams. So, on that level, there's less connectivity. But, I'm getting way more done, have less distractions and more focus, plus I have less travel time. In addition to getting more work done in the breaks, I can do a couple of loads of washing, I can contribute to dinner or whatever. And that makes me feel I'm on top of things and family life is humming.

Other opportunities to improve productivity include office space with different work places that suit different activities/work styles that suit people. We have done this recently at EY with our new office which is all open plan and has meeting rooms, quiet areas, team work zones etc. This is great for connectivity, and when people are connected I think their general sense of well-being is better and their productivity increases.

Work needs to be a place that people want to come to, feel they belong, their values align with those of the company and the individuals are valued. Even if the person loves the technical / task element of their job, if they don't have these other things, then I don't think their productivity is being maximised.

There will always be elements of unproductivity in a workforce, because when people come to work, they need to be able to do a bit of this and a bit of that. They need to be able to have a coffee and have a chat. Part of the work environment and feeling good about yourself as a human being is social interaction, belonging to a team. So, you can't say those elements are unproductive, because it's about human well-being, which is all part of contributing to better productivity in the long run.

How do you manage your communication, including your inbox, ensuring you have the right balance between effective communication and management of your time? Is email management a challenge for you?

That's a good question, because the emails are constantly coming in and seem to be increasing. I get virtually no calls on the landline. Communication is phone calls to mobiles, lots of texts but, by far the majority is email. Most clients will send a quick email if they need to contact me. The volume of emails is excessive some days, which I think is about poor protocol amongst individuals. You're cc'd in absolutely everything—which to me, at times, is the individual covering their backside in case something goes wrong. So, letting teams know that if I am cc'd that I believe I am not expected to respond to their email and indeed may not get to it.

In my diary, I have a couple of half-hour blocks per day, which is my catch up on emails time. And then, there is usually checking at the end of the day. In between meetings, if I have the opportunity to check emails, I will delete or forward on for action. But anything I need to take action on gets done during the half-hour time blocks.

Any email I'm cc'd on is filtered differently; it is given lower priority. If an email is addressed to me, I'll look at that first; cc emails I treat as 'for your information only.'

I also think there needs to be etiquette rules around use of phones (to check emails) in meetings. My personal view is: when you're in a meeting, you don't look at your phone. If I am expecting something urgent via email, then I let those in the meeting know that at the beginning of the meeting.

In terms of after-hours checking of emails– I check emails up to a certain time of the evening, which can vary depending on what is going on, but most times that is up to 7 pm. I don't check emails for at least thirty minutes before I go to bed to enable me to unwind and to go to sleep. No emails or phones during meal time at home. This applies to the whole family.

Habits and routines – what are some of your habits and routines that are key to your life balance and success?

I have a number of positive habits.

I am in the house for breakfast with the kids before school, I do drop offs and most days I don't get into the office before 9 am.

Diary management which I spoke about earlier is vital to time management at work. Being organised and getting the key dates in the calendar for important events for my husband and kids. Ensuring I have slots in the diary every day for the unexpected that come up.

I have rules around my inbox and try to stick to my rules around when I check emails when at home. This includes not looking at the phone for at least half an hour before I go to sleep.

It takes a lot for me to be in the office now at 7pm, other than when there is an urgent deadline.

I get at least 7 hours of sleep a night, as I think sleep deprivation for most means lack of focus, lack of productivity and generally not feeling great.

Spending time with my kids on the weekend doing what they want to do, their sport, helping with homework, being at home for dinner on week nights for most nights in the week, spending time with my husband doing things we enjoy like together and friends are also healthy habits.

I have a few bad habits too. One is the minute I get up in the morning, I grab my phone and that's a bad habit. My other bad habit (that I'm getting better at) is looking at emails whilst I'm moving. I did go through a period when I was doing emails in the car; I've stopped that now. The habit that I'm trying to stop now is walking through the city on the pavement and doing emails. You sub-consciously know you're crossing the street, but it's just so dangerous.

Flexibility – what are your thoughts on flexibility within the workforce, including flexible hours and working from home?

I think flexibility is going to become even more important, because if you want good people, many of them will want a flexible working life. I think we've just got to get smarter at the way we enable those people to get the flexibility they desire. In the whole world of connectivity today, we have the ability to set up at home or wherever. The winners in business will be the people who can think outside the box. They are okay with their employees not sitting around them every single day.

EY keeps timesheets, so it's a very easy mechanism for ensuring people are working—wherever that may be. For organisations that don't have timesheets, there is a risk around that. But, I think there will always be elements of that; it's human nature. But, you know, they could be sitting at work and be incredibly unproductive. Just because they are present, doesn't mean they are productive. People seem to judge people on the hours they've worked, rather than on the value created, the output they've created; and that needs to change.

Employers who support flexible hours or working from home, for employees who want that, I think will win in the quest for talent retention.

Top tips/takeaways – what are your tips/takeaways for success?

The first one is to believe in yourself. You must back yourself. Be true to yourself, because there will always be other people judging you. You've got to be strong and just say, "I don't need to justify what I'm doing, and nor will I judge other people." That then is a big part of having strength of character (and strength in your own mind about what's right for you and your family) and dealing with some of those tougher days.

Don't blame yourself; don't beat yourself up, because there are going to be days which are not good days. Often, women blame themselves if something goes wrong at home. An example is: if your child's grades are dropping. Men have bad days too, but generally, they don't beat themselves up. Or if they do, they don't visibly do. And don't sweat the small stuff.

Another tip would be to have at least one person somewhere in your life that is a coach or mentor. Whether it's the flexibility piece, a situation at work, a situation at home, whatever it happens to be, that they can support you through with their advice — I'm a believer that someone somewhere has dealt with this before, who can help you through the situation.

More broadly, you need to have a good support network. The support you have at home must be working to help you, or else you're going to be a square peg in a round hole all the time. And that's an awful way to get through your daily life.

And lastly you must be clear what you want to achieve, so you have clarity around your goals. This clarity will allow you to direct your focus and energy for both work and your home life and will ultimately help you achieve the integration of work and life that works for you.

21

Interview – Catriona Noble, Managing Director Retail Distribution, ANZ

As Managing Director Retail Distribution, ANZ, Catriona Noble leads over 6,000 people supporting over five million customers. She is responsible for all retail distribution channels, including the branch network, mobile lending, brokers, customer contact centre, ATMs and wealth direct distribution.

Prior to joining ANZ in 2015, Catriona was Chief Restaurant Officer, Asia, Pacific, Middle East and Africa for the McDonald's Corporation with responsibility for over 10,000 restaurants and 200,000 people. This followed over twenty years with McDonald's Australia, including four years as CEO and Managing Director.

Catriona completed the Business and Economics Advanced Management Programme at INSEAD business school. She is a member and mentor with the Business Council of Australia and Deputy Chair of the National Place Based Advisory Group on the Australian Social Inclusion Board.

What is your definition of work-life balance and how do you manage it?

I don't think you're ever in balance. At any one moment of time, you're always out of balance. The way I like to think of it is more like juggling. So, you're constantly trying to juggle all these different parts of your life, and sometimes you drop a ball—and that's okay. At some point, you will pick it up again. For me, the important thing is not dropping it for too long.

There might be periods where everything ebbs and flows. You might have periods where you spend more time at work, because of what's going on. But, when there's the opportunity, you pull back. So, you might have a month where you are a bit frantic; however, the next month you need to give more time to your family—or to yourself for your own health. It can't be that I'll get to it in a few years. It's got to be constant, regular juggling.

What do you consider some of the greatest challenges that employees working in an office environment face today?

I think it's important that all our staff feel they have a sense of purpose; they can see why they're coming to work, which is particularly important in large organisations like ANZ. How do they fit into it, and how do they contribute?

And I think that's an imperative for each individual—to feel engaged, to feel fulfilled, and to go home thinking: Okay, I made a difference today. It is critical to the success of the organization as well. We talk about people at the front line needing to do a good job, but it's never just about the front line. There's so many pieces of an upstream that must go right. So, helping our people in the back and the middle office to have visibility—and line of sight right through to the customer, and see how they fit in—is a real challenge.

There are very different dynamics of people that are out in the banking network, versus people that are based in the office. They all have challenges but they're different. So, there is pressure when you're in a frontline role; a lot of times, your time is not your own, because you're being responsive to customer flow. And you don't always feel like you can control the situation; if things don't go right during the day, then yes, quite often those people are waiting until—say the branch is shut, and then they've got to stay and get a whole lot of work done. So, that's always a challenge.

In the office, there's a different type of pressure, because there is always a level of judgment. If you're quite efficient with your work, and hence work shorter hours than the people around you, then there can be a judgment around your performance. It's crazy in today's environment that presentism is still an issue; but, I think it is. And, I have noticed it even more so in banking. You do have a lot of office-based people, and there is this sense of people watching what kind of hours you are doing. Even though we talk about flexibility, it's real—and we have lots of people working part time and working from home—but, there is still the sense of being present.

How we change that perception is a tough question. It's a tough one, because how do you evaluate somebody's work and their output? So often, you'll evaluate what you can observe, which is the amount of effort put in. And, as we know, that doesn't always correlate with output, productivity and efficiency.

I think a lot of places are experimenting with different things around peer reviews and so on, and some people seem to be even getting rid of performance reviews. Reviews are something, but they're not perfect. It's still a judgment. I don't have a definitive answer; I just think the workplace is going to continue to evolve. And the traditional methods of evaluating productivity and defining people's performance level are going to be challenged; and is there even going to be a rating for someone's performance that correlates with what remuneration they receive? I just wonder: are people going to be assessed more on their reputation? So, will people not even be in this traditional notion of a role? Will everyone almost become a contractor, a freelancer? So, therefore, what matters is what people truly think of your work. Do they want you to do more work for them or not? Maybe they won't worry about labelling it.

Communication – how do you manage your communication, including your inbox, ensuring you have the right balance between effective communication and management of your time? Is email management a challenge for you?

I know there are some people who say they like to switch off from technology, but I think it's just life now. There's no work-life balance. I like having a smartphone, and I will regularly look at my emails and just clear them. Otherwise, you come to a barrage. A lot of things you can just delete straight away, or you can forward to the appropriate person for action.

Probably once a week, and often just when I'm sitting at home one night, I'll change my email view—sorted by person rather than by date—so, I can look at them in blocks and clarify what I haven't actioned, what I need to follow up on, or what I can delete now. I try not to agonize every day too much over email. I try to look at what I need to action, pop it on my to-do list, as something I need to read or be aware of. Sometimes, it's things that are relevant for an upcoming meeting; and so, having a good EA is great, because she'll often take that content and attach it to the calendar invite (and it's there where it's meant to be). And then you can get rid of the actual email.

I don't have issues managing the volume of emails. When I have a spare five minutes, whether that be between meetings, I'll check my email. I just try to keep on top of it.

The communication from my team isn't more email or phone or text; it's a combination. It takes a little while to work out what works best, a little while to find a routine, a rhythm with a new team. It's also about understanding how people like to work. I know with some people, I can just call them and they'll pretty much always pick up their phone, and other people seem to be averse to the phone. So, I'll either text them or email them; and then with some of my colleagues, I'll need to email their EAs to schedule a phone call. If I just call them, I'm highly unlikely to get them, and they are highly unlikely to return my call. It's just not the way they work.

It's not enough to have your own way of doing things; you need to get to know how your key stakeholders work and determine the most efficient way to work together. I used to get annoyed when people didn't return calls, and then I realised that it's not personal. They just don't check their voicemail; it's just not how they work. If I want to have a conversation with them, and I want to have a good working relationship with them, then it's no point being annoyed. It's about finding another way.

Flexibility – what are your thoughts on flexibility within the workforce, including flexible hours and working from home?

It's unique to each person's position. If, for example, our Contact Centre Manager wanted to work from home, it would be difficult—because they've got to constantly be there, visible with their teams. They've got to be listening in on calls and giving feedback. However, if it was some of my other team members, there is quite a bit of work that they can do from home—not exclusively though, because they're all in leadership roles, so they need to be face-to-face with their teams. Flexibility could increase if there were less meetings.

Habits and routines – what are some of your habits and routines that are key to your life balance and success?

I take the 6.30 am flight from Sydney to Melbourne. There's something about getting up before 5 am which just doesn't work for me, and I suspect many others.

As I mentioned previously, I consider scheduling key catch-ups for the entire year, including my own team and times with my children, as a habit.

I'm very disciplined around keeping to the schedule that includes sticking to start times and end times. I insist on meetings or presentations not rehashing the pre-read. Face-to-face time should be value-adding.

I have a daily to-do list that sets my priorities for the day; that's another habit.

Productivity – what are the areas of opportunity in the productivity arena that you routinely witness and experience?

There is a lot of real receptiveness to saying we need to do business differently and we need to evolve. It's not so much what we are going to start doing—people are okay with that; it's letting go of certain things that we need to stop doing is where it sometimes gets hard, because people get scared. They've been conditioned over a long period of time that we must do these certain things. It's trying to get people to let go of some of those things, and say it's not about compromising our integrity or undermining our risk culture. It's about finding a better way to do it; it's about substance over form.

Quite a lot of things that we do in the bank, I believe, are a lot about form and paperwork. And, I constantly challenge the team to say how that has reduced the risk, improved customer outcomes and improved banker outcomes. And if they can't answer that, then we can challenge this.

I think one of the big issues we have around productivity (or output and people's own sense of frustration around getting things done) is this culture around meetings. If everyone was working whatever hours from whatever location, how do you have meetings? We over-rely on meetings. Meetings are a very effective way of conducting a deep intervention into something, but they are completely over-used. People acknowledge that there are too many meetings, but they don't see an alternative.

When I was based in Singapore with McDonald's, my team was spread out across Asia Pacific. So, everybody was working remotely; everyone accommodated each other. And, I just think we were so much more productive—and we couldn't just meet every week, for say, four hours. We'd do it on the phone or on video conference; and you just can't run all day meetings that way. We did have some face-to-face meetings, but they were a lot less frequent; and they were very valued. So, you think about what's going to be on the agenda; and, how you're going to make the best of this time?

I'm encouraging my team to challenge the meetings they're in— and just stop going to some. A couple of meetings ago, I got someone to get everyone's diaries and find anywhere there were two levels of people in the same meeting. And then I said to my team, "You either need to empower the person at the lower level to go to the meeting, and make the decisions; or, you need to go, but then, they shouldn't be there." So, I was just challenging some of these notions about the double-up of these things as well. So just constantly question: do you have to be in that meeting? Does the meeting even need to happen?

What are your secrets/tips/techniques for success in life balance?

I try to schedule a lot of the framework of what I know from experience is important. So, you might think it's nice to be very impromptu with your staff, to catch up. But, I plan a whole year of catch ups with my staff. The time will depend on how experienced they are, how long they've been in the role and what their role is. But, as a minimum, I schedule half an hour every month—and an hour every quarter. Again, depending on their role, I'll have time out in the field with them. But, it's always there as a minimum. And of course, I talk to them a lot more than half an hour a month, but that's just the absolute minimum.

For home, I create a skeleton diary—which I can then add to other than the non-negotiables; the most important things go in first. I must admit it's not part of my current routine, but I did regularly go to the gym, so that time would go into my diary. I do my kids' sports, so that's always in my diary as a priority.

I try to pick up on little things that make a difference in my kids' lives. It doesn't always have to be the big event. For example, yesterday I left early because my daughter was a little bit stressed with everything she has going on. So, I picked her up from the library at five, just so she didn't have the hassle of catching the bus. I lot of people talk about missing the big events with their children, whether that be a swimming carnival or whatever. Occasionally, I'll go to those things, but not all the time, because I'd rather prioritise making time, for sometimes, the little things. With the little things, it's the real opportunity to connect.

Life balance is different for everybody, but it's finding those little things, particularly things that are important to you. So, for some people, their health and fitness is important. And, while it's important to me, it probably doesn't rank Number One. It's kind of doing enough to be healthy. I'd love to weigh five kilograms less, but it's not the A priority for me, as long as I'm healthy. And connection with family is also really important—touching base with my extended family, my brother and my sister and my mother-in-law.

References

Web

Feldman, Loren. "Today's Must-Reads For Entrepreneurs: Saving BlackBerry." Forbes. May 23, 2016.http://www.forbes.com/sites/lorenfeldman/2016/05/23/todays-must-reads-for-entrepreneurs-saving-blackberry/.

Bloom, Nicholas. "To Raise Productivity, Let More Employees Work from Home." Harvard Business Review. August 21, 2014. https://hbr.org/2014/01/to-raise-productivity-let-more-employees-work-from-home.

Chung, Frank. "Sweden embraces six-hour workday." News Limited. October 02, 2015.http://www.news.com.au/finance/work/at-work/sweden-embraces-the-sixhour-work-day/news-story/567817e54b33509730e2400d04c2dbd9.

Ware, Bronnie. "REGRETS OF THE DYING." bronnieware.com. November 16, 2015.http://bronnieware.com/regrets-of-the-dying/.

Greenfield, Rebecca. "The Six-Hour Workday Works in Europe. What About America?" Bloomberg.com. May 10, 2016.http://www.bloomberg.com/news/articles/2016-05-10/the-six-hour-workday-works-in-europe-what-about-america.

CareerJunction. "Shorter Workweek Good For Companies." CareerJunction Blog. May 18, 2016.http://www.careerjunction.co.za/blog/?p=32360.

"Ford factory workers get 40-hour week." History.com.http://www.history.com/this-day-in-history/ford-factory-workers-get-40-hour-week.

Alderman, Liz. "In Sweden, an Experiment Turns Shorter Workdays into Bigger Gains." ACQ5. May 20, 2016.http://www.acq5.com/post/in-sweden-an-experiment-turns-shorter-workdays-into-bigger-gains/.

Widrich, Leonhard. "The Origin of the 8 Hour Work Day and Why We Should Rethink It." The Huffington Post. January 07, 2014; updated November 22, 2016.http://www.huffingtonpost.com/leonhard-widrich/the-origin-of-the-8-hour-_b_4524488.html.

Stott, Phil. "Are We Heading for a 6-Hour Workday?" CLS Legal Staffing. May 24, 2016.http://clslegalstaffing.com/articles/are-we-heading-6-hour-workday.

Neese, Brian. "Working Remotely Works." Rivier University Online. October 14, 2015.http://online.rivier.edu/working-remotely-works/.

Writer, TFPP, Robert Gehl, and C.E. Dyer. "Why Democrats' Version of History of Unions Is All Wrong." The Federalist Papers. May 02, 2016.http://thefederalistpapers.org/us/why-democrats-version-of-history-of-unions-is-all-wrong.

Greenfield, Rebecca. "The six-hour work day increases productivity. So will Britain and America adopt one?" The Independent. June 0 2016.http://www.independent.co.uk/news/business/the-six-hour-work-day-increases-productivity-so-will-britain-and-america-adopt-one-sweden-a7066961.html.

Monks, Kieron. "Introducing the 20-hour work week." CNN. October 28, 2015.http://www.cnn.com/2015/10/28/world/twenty-hour-work-week/index.html.

Bloom, Nicholas, and Scott Berinato. "To raise productivity, let more employees work from home." TODAYonline. March 21, 2014.http://www.todayonline.com/singapore/raise-productivity-let-more-employees-work-home.

Cole, Samantha. "Working From Home Is Awesome--If You Do It Right." Fast Company. July 07, 2014.https://www.fastcompany.com/3032648/work-smart/working-from-home-is-awesome-if-you-do-it-right.

Greenfield, Rebecca. "The six-hour workday works in Sweden. But what about in workaholic North America?" Financial Post. May 11, 2016.http://business.financialpost.com/executive/careers/the-six-hour-workday-works-in-sweden-but-what-about-in-workaholic-north-america.

Steiner, Susie. "Top five regrets of the dying." The Guardian. February 01, 2012.https://www.theguardian.com/lifeandstyle/2012/feb/01/top-five-regrets-of-the-dying.

Miller, Tessa. "Why We Should Rethink the Eight-Hour Workday." Lifehacker. June 20, 2013.http://lifehacker.com/why-we-should-rethink-the-eight-hour-workday-515742249.

"ADVO Group interviews Andreas Konig, CEO at TeamViewer."
HR PMI Employee Benefit News.http://news.advogroup.co.uk/
advo-group-interviews-andreas-konig-ceo-at-teamviewer/.

Henderson, Adam. "Workplace trust for flexible working."
Millennial Mindset. April 29, 2016.http://millennialmindset.
co.uk/if-you-cant-trust-your-employees-to-work-flexibly-why-
hire-them-in-the-first-place/.

Alderman, Liz. "Shorter workdays equal greater efficiency in
Swedish experiment." Financial Review. May 23, 2016.http://
www.afr.com/news/economy/employment/shorter-workdays-
equal-greater-efficiency-in-swedish-experiment-20160522-gp0s8i.

Rosen, Katerina. "The Top 5 Regrets Of The Dying." The
Huffington Post. August 03, 2013.http://www.huffingtonpost.
com/2013/08/03/top-5-regrets-of-the-dying_n_3640593.html.

Clifford, Catherine. "Why Amazon and other companies are
trying 30-hour workweeks." CNBC. September 16, 2016.http://
www.cnbc.com/2016/09/16/why-amazon-and-other-companies-
are-trying-30-hour-workweeks.html.

Brinkley, Douglas. "The 40-Hour Revolution." Time Inc.
March 31, 2003.http://content.time.com/time/specials/packages/
article/0,28804,1977881_1977883_1977922,00.html.

Caprino, Cathy. "Five Reasons You're Killing Yourself Working
Overtime, and How to Stop." Forbes. April 30, 2015.http://
www.forbes.com/sites/kathycaprino/2015/04/30/5-reasons-youre-
killing-yourself-working-overtime-and-how-to-stop/.

Fisher, Sharon. "Employees Looking for Better Work-Life Balance." Laserfiche. April 20, 2015.https://www.laserfiche.com/simplicity/employees-looking-for-better-work-life-balance/.

Clark, Dorrie. "Using the 80/20 Principle to Improve Your Productivity and Happiness." Dorie Clark.http://dorieclark.com/using-the-8020-principle-to-improve-your-productivity-and-happiness/.

Bonne, Emily. "How to Prioritize Your To-Dos When Everything's Important." Wrike. July 23, 2015.https://www.wrike.com/blog/how-to-prioritize-when-everythings-important-video/.

McKay, Brett & Kate. "The Eisenhower Decision Matrix: How to Distinguish Between Urgent and Important Tasks and Make Real Progress in Your Life." The Art of Manliness. October 23,2013.http://www.artofmanliness.com/2013/10/23/eisenhower-decision-matrix/.

Nesdale, Sheldon. "My notes on *The 80/20 Principle: The Secret of Achieving More with Less* by Robert Koch." LoveBusinessBooks. February 17, 2009.http://www.lovebusinessbooks.com/2009/02/the-8020-principle-the-secret-of-achieving-more-with-less-by-richard-koch/.

Vaccaro, Pamela J. "The 80/20 Rule of Time Management."American Academy of Family Practice Physicians. *Family Practice Management*, September 2000. http://www.aafp.org/fpm/2000/0900/p76.html.

Radwan, M. Farouk. "Inspirational stories of successful people." To Know Myself.https://www.2knowmyself.com/inspirational_stories_of_successful_and_famous_people.

Cousens, Caleb. "3 Productivity Killers for Bloggers." Social Media Wizard. May 17, 2016.http://www.socialmediawizard.com/2016/05/17/productivity-killers/.

Betterhealth.vic.gov.au. "Breakfast." Department of Health & Human Services, State Government of Victoria, Australia.https://www.betterhealth.vic.gov.au/health/healthyliving/breakfast.

Adams, R. L. "12 Famous People Who Failed Before Succeeding." Wanderlust Worker,https://www.wanderlustworker.com/12-famous-people-who-failed-before-succeeding/.

Forleo, Marie. "The Secret to More Meaning & Adventure W/Chris Guillebeau." Marie Forleo.http://www.marieforleo.com/2014/09/happiness-of-pursuit/.

Moon, Jerred. "If You're Not Failing, You're Not Trying." End of Three Fitness.http://www.endofthreefitness.com/if-youre-not-failing-youre-not-trying/.

Winfield, Chris. "The Ultimate Guide to Becoming Your Best Self: Build Your Daily Routine by Optimizing Your Mind, Body and Spirit." Buffer Inc. September 21, 2015.https://open.buffer.com/daily-success-routine/.

Ciotti, Gregory. "5 Scientific Ways to Build Habits That Stick." 99u.http://99u.com/articles/17123/5-scientific-ways-to-build-habits-that-stick.

Kjerulf, Alexander. "Top 10 Reasons Why Happiness at Work Is the Ultimate Productivity Booster." The Chief Happiness Officer Blog. March 27, 2007.http://positivesharing.com/2007/03/

top-10-reasons-why-happiness-at-work-is-the-ultimate-productivity-booster/.

Duffy, Jill. "Get Organized: 11 Tips for Managing Email." PCMag UK. March 5, 2012.http://uk.pcmag.com/e-mail-products/65853/feature/get-organized-11-tips-for-managing-email.

Bradberry, Travis. "10 Harsh Lessons That Will Make You More Successful." Entrepreneur Media, Inc. October 18, 2016.https://www.entrepreneur.com/article/283726.

Lewis, Michael. "Obama's Way." *Vanity Fair*. October 2012. http://www.aafp.org/fpm/2000/0900/p76.html.

Clear, James. "The 3 R's of Habit Change: How to Start New Habits That Actually Stick." James Clear.http://jamesclear.com/three-steps-habit-change.

Young, Scott H. "18 Tricks to Make New Habits Stick." Lifehack. http://www.lifehack.org/articles/featured/18-tricks-to-make-new-habits-stick.html.

Unstuck.com. "How We Procrastinate (and May Not Even Know It)." Unstuck LLC.https://www.unstuck.com/how-we-procrastinate/.

Clear, James. "How to Stop Procrastinating by Using the 2-Minute Rule." James Clear.http://jamesclear.com/how-to-stop-procrastinating.

Babauta, Leo. "The Amazing Power of Being Present." Zen Habits. August 12, 2011.https://zenhabits.net/mindful/.

Wikipedia. "Flow." Modified January 3, 2017.https://en.wikipedia. org/wiki/Flow_(psychology).

Seiter, Courtney. "The Science of Taking Breaks at Work: How to Be More Productive by Changing the Way You Think About Downtime." Buffer Inc. March 23, 2015.https://open.buffer.com/ science-taking-breaks-at-work/.

Schwartz, Tony and McCarthy, Catherine. "Manage Your Energy, Not Your Time." Harvard Business Review. October 2007 issue. https://hbr.org/2007/10/manage-your-energy-not-your-time.

Bradberry, Travis. "Multitasking Damages Your Brain and Your Career, New Studies Suggest." Talentsmart.http://www. talentsmart.com/articles/Multitasking-Damages-Your-Brain-and-Your-Career,-New-Studies-Suggest-2102500909-p-1.html.

Wikipedia. "Pygmalion effect." Modified January 6, 2017.https:// en.wikipedia.org/wiki/Pygmalion_effect.

Kim, Larry. "Multitasking Is Killing Your Brain." Inc.com. July 15, 2015.http://www.inc.com/larry-kim/why-multi-tasking-is-killing-your-brain.html.

Mindtools.com. "Overcoming Procrastination." Mind Tools Ltd. https://www.mindtools.com/pages/article/newHTE_96.htm.

Paech, Gemma. "Why it's time to stop hitting the snooze button." World Economic Forum. January 7, 2015.https://www.weforum.org/ agenda/2015/01/why-its-time-to-stop-hitting-the-snooze-button/.

MacMillan, Amanda. "Multitasking Is a Don't: 12 Reasons to Stop Doing It." Awaken. June 15, 2013.http://www.awaken. com/2013/06/multitasking-is-a-dont-12-reasons-to-stop-doing-it/.

Spira, Johnathan & Feintuch, Joshua. "The Cost of Not Paying Attention: How Interruptions Impact Knowledge Worker Productivity." Basex. September 2005.http://iorgforum.org/ wp-content/uploads/2011/06/CostOfNotPayingAttention. BasexReport1.pdf.

Lifehacker. "5 Rules of Email Management You Should Adopt." Lifehacker UK. February 18, 2015.http://www.lifehacker. co.uk/2015/02/18/5-rules-email-management-adopt.

Kruse, Kevin. "The 3 Secrets to Leaving the Office by 5 O'Clock—Guilt Free." Mujojoma Dioméde. November 10, 2015. https://mujojoma.wordpress.com/2015/11/10/the-3-secrets-to-leaving-the-office-by-5-oclock-guilt-free/.

Ecker, Ddiana. "15Tips for Managing Email Overload at Work." Redbooth. July 15, 2015. https://redbooth.com/blog/managing-email-overload.

Weiner, Jeff. LinkedIn CEO: How I manage my email." Quartz. August 5, 2013.http://qz.com/111891/linkedin-ceo-how-i-manage-my-email/.

Lyttle, J. and Baugh, E. "The Importance of Family Dinners." University of Florida IFAS Extension.http://solutionsforyourlife. ufl.edu/hot_topics/families_and_consumers/family_dinners. shtml.

Du, Frances. "Why You Shouldn't Feel Guilty About Leaving work at 5:00." Culture-ist. October 17, 2012.http://www.thecultureist. com/2012/10/17/work-life-balance-leaving-work-at-5/.

MacMillan, Amanda. "5 Weird Ways Stress Can Actually Be Good for You." Time Inc. August 22, 2014.http://time. com/3162088/5-weird-ways-stress-can-actually-be-good-for-you/.

Fishel, Anne. "The most important thing you can do with your kids? Eat dinner with them." The Washington Post. January 12, 2015.https://www.washingtonpost.com/posteverything/ wp/2015/01/12/the-most-important-thing-you-can-do-with-your-kids-eat-dinner-with-them/.

Donovan, Laura. "Sheryl Sandberg Leaves Work at 5:30 Every day—and You Should Too." Mashable. April 5, 2012.http:// mashable.com/2012/04/05sheryl-sandberg-leaves-work-at-530#6UWiP4Ue3aqU.

Gratias, Melissa. "The Intriguing Psychology Behind CC-ing People on Emails." Redbooth. May 26, 2016.https://redbooth. com/blog/email-cc-psychology.

Goop.com. "Why Stress Is Actually Good for Us—and How to Get good at It: A Q&A with Kelly McGonigal." Goop.http://goop.com/ why-stress-is-actually-good-for-us-and-how-to-get-good-at-it/.

Quotes

Quotes not taken from above referenced articles are sourced from: https://www.goodreads.com/quotes.

Books

Ferriss, Timothy. *The 4-hour workweek: escape 9-5, live anywhere, and join the new rich.* New York: Crown Publishers, 2009.

Covey, Stephen R. *The 7 habits of highly effective people.* Provo, UT: Franklin Covey, 1998.

Grove, Andrew S. *High output management.* New York: Vintage, 1995.

Fishel, Anne K. *Home for dinner: mixing food, fun, and conversation for a happier family and healthier kids.* New York: American Management Association, 2015.

Koran, Al. *Bring out the magic in your mind.* Wellingborough, Northamptonshire: Thorsons, 1972.

Koch, Richard. *The 80/20 principle*: London: Nicholas Brealey Publishing, 1998

Printed in Australia
AUOC01n1319140617
286659AU00002B/4/P

9 781504 307628